THE SPIRITUAL PRACTICE OF REMEMBERING

The Spiritual Practice of Remembering

MARGARET BENDROTH

WILLIAM B. EERDMANS PUBLISHING COMPANY
GRAND RAPIDS, MICHIGAN / CAMBRIDGE, U.K.

Published 2013 by
Wm. B. Eerdmans Publishing Co.
2140 Oak Industrial Drive N.E., Grand Rapids, Michigan 49505 /
P.O. Box 163, Cambridge CB3 9PU U.K.

Library of Congress Cataloging-in-Publication Data

Bendroth, Margaret Lamberts, 1954-
The spiritual practice of remembering / Margaret Bendroth.
    pages   cm
Includes bibliographical references.
ISBN 978-0-8028-6897-8 (pbk.   )
1. Memory — Religious aspects — Christianity.   I. Title.

BV4597.565.B46   2013
248.4'6 — dc23

                    2013020949

www.eerdmans.com

To All the Saints
  at First Church,
    Cambridge, Massachusetts

Contents

ACKNOWLEDGMENTS   viii

INTRODUCTION: On Keeping and Tossing   1

1. Stranded in the Present   13

2. Past Imperfect   31

3. Memory Loss   54

4. The Great Conversation   76

5. The Communion of Saints   99

6. The Spiritual Practice of Remembering   120

Acknowledgments

This book began with a Project Grant from the Louisville Institute, and took shape in conversations at the Winter Seminar in 2011. Many thanks to Jim Lewis and the other participants who offered some timely new ideas and the encouragement I needed. The background scholarship and a lot of the research took place over the course of a sabbatical granted by the American Congregational Association, the historic non-profit organization that runs the Congregational Library, and is my employer.

Thank you also to the Library staff who have accommodated my strange writing schedule over these months and years: Claudette, Cary, Jessica, Robin, Cristina, Alex, and Steven. I am thankful also to Suchesta, John, George, David, and the Beacon Street football pool.

I am grateful to the family and friends who have given me space to write and think, and who have kept me from taking myself too seriously. Thank you Norman, Nathan, and Anna. Thanks also to Ken Orth and all the Friday Night Theologues: Tony, Karen, Nancy, Mary, Ann, Kate, and Don.

THIS BOOK IS DEDICATED to the communion of saints at First Church in Cambridge, Massachusetts, of which I am a part. In 2011 they celebrated their 375th anniversary as a congregation, an event which did more to teach me what history might mean than all the books in my library. For all those saints, from 1636 onward, I am deeply grateful.

On Keeping and Tossing

One chilly winter Sunday I walked up the steps of a small New England church, and into a set of questions I have been thinking about ever since.

Part of my job as director of the Congregational Library, an old Boston institution in the heart of Beacon Hill, is visiting local churches. In fact, a lot of my responsibilities are ceremonial: I give talks at anniversary services or sermons for "history Sunday," and I have been guest of honor at more church suppers than I can recall, from Maine to Washington State. My task is to remind people that they are part of a much larger story, one that began with the New England Puritans and still continues today. And somehow, despite all the watery coffee and starchy church food, that part of my job never gets old.

These trips are always an adventure, especially for someone with a historian's training and, I admit, instinct for prying. But this one was unusual from the start. Even by New England standards this particular church had a long past, with deep Puritan roots and a few famous pastors. In fact, one of them was already very familiar to me: he looks down from an oil portrait mounted high on the wall of our turn-of-the-century reading room — not very happily, I should add.

After a while I learned not to take this personally, and as a gesture of good will I came with a few anecdotes about him to share with the congregation. And so, as a group of us stood together in the narthex, I launched into a story about how the famous reverend would arrive at church on Sundays, stepping down from a large carriage, all dressed in black. He was a small man and made up for his deficiency in size with an intimidating presence. As the story goes, the congregation would part like the waters of the Red Sea as he marched down the aisle and up into his pulpit holding a very large black tricorne hat against his chest.

"Why, there it is right there!" one of the group broke in. I turned around and saw that very same hat, now much the worse for wear, sitting in a small Plexiglas box right below a large window. It was slowly baking to death in the sunlight.

Fortunately, my hosts interpreted my gasp of dismay as one of awe. One of them even offered to let me take it back to the Library, though I declined politely. Unless someone was interested in eighteenth-century millinery, the hat had relatively little to offer any of our researchers. I also added a few suggestions about better places for the display than under a window.

On my way home, I could not stop wondering what that poor old tricorne hat was doing in the entry hall of a Protestant church. I have visited enough Roman Catholic churches to be familiar with reliquaries, made to hold the sacred memorabilia of saints and church fathers, and I had been to plenty of museums that displayed everything imaginable from the colonial era, from clay pipes and pottery shards to underwear and old shoes. But something different seemed to be going on here, and the question would not go away: what did those Yankee Protestants see when they passed by that Plexiglas case every Sunday?

Probably to most of them it was just an odd curio, a silent reminder of a mercifully bygone past, when ministers aimed to intimidate their flocks rather than sip coffee with them in the fellowship hall. Others might have seen the tricorne hat as a kind of a totem, almost like a magic amulet offering protection against outside forces. A few would have seen it as a testimony to the perseverance of the old saints through difficult times.

I knew beyond a doubt, however, that the Plexiglas reliquary would have irritated the hat's original owner no end. Like many Congregational ministers of his day, he was fiercely opposed to anything that smacked of ritual, including the keeping of relics. The old eighteenth-century meetinghouse he presided over would have been as stark and plain as the theology he thundered from his pulpit. And nothing would have horrified him more than to see his hat living on in a plastic case – long after his ardent Calvinism had fallen by the cultural wayside.

So why keep it? And for that matter, why hold onto anything old and no longer useful?

The Power of Old Things

Certainly that tricorne hat survived because it was, in some way, wonderful. There is something awe-inspiring about an object that is indescribably and incredibly old. A three-hundred-year-old devotional book in my Rare Book Room is, on the one hand, just ancient paper and ink in an old binding in need of careful preservation. But it is also an object of mystery. Perhaps a minister pored over it by candlelight or a father read it aloud to his family, sitting around the fire after a long day of work in the fields. It might have belonged to someone who died in war or who was lost at sea. Sometimes the owners wrote their names across the title page, in careful and uneven script, and sometimes they underlined or commented on the text. But these clues only raise more questions about what moved those readers in the first place – not just to underline the text, but to buy the book itself.

We are not just talking about books, of course. That much becomes obvious with any trip through a church archive, where oddities stare down from every shelf. The Methodist library at Drew University, for example, is the memory receptacle for one of the most plainspoken and simple forms of American Protestantism, yet it boasts a collection of relics that would do the Vatican proud: a scrap of fabric from one of John Wesley's clothes, a piece of velvet upholstery fabric from a chair he owned, and a wooden peg from a Methodist church where his fellow evangelist Francis Asbury once hung his coat. The collection even includes an oddly-shaped black object, said to be the tip of the thumb of eighteenth-century evangelist George Whitefield.[1] My Congregationalists were a bit more prosaic in their collecting habits, but we certainly have our share of rocks (in our case from Plymouth), furniture sat upon by semi-famous people, and unidentified pieces of fabric and coins. I am certainly not immune to the lure of old things: the flotsam and jetsam in my office includes a two-hundred-year-old brick from the Park Street Church, a souvenir calendar featuring famous Congregationalist Henry Ward Beecher, and many piles of old tracts, Sunday school buttons, and commemorative coins.

I suspect that in some mysterious and compelling way those old objects point us to the unseen. Even more, they form an emotional bridge to the now-invisible people who made them long ago. A brick from a demolished church building has the power to evoke feelings of sadness, joy, and regret. Even one of the old chairs in my library has the metaphorical power to raise the dead, at least in the memory and imagination, as I wonder about its original owner, Jonathan Edwards Jr., and what his world was like. We could

---

1. Colleen McDannell, *Material Christianity: Religion and Popular Culture in America* (New Haven: Yale University Press, 1995), pp. 42-43.

say that in some sense they are holy – things that are special and set apart from ordinary use.

In this sense remembering is an act with spiritual meaning, pushing us against the unknown. True, it has all kinds of practical value, especially when we need to find the way home or come up with the name of the person standing in front of us. But there is another dimension. Thinking back through time can be like reaching into dark, murky water with no idea of what your hands will come across: a lovely shell or something with spines and venom. Remembering, like all matters spiritual, requires imagination, trust, and courage.

It is also deeply woven into the religious faith we have inherited. Both Christianity and Judaism are fundamentally "religions of remembrance," as historian Jacques Le Goff writes.[2] Thousands of years ago the Jewish people came to know God, not through a set of abstract philosophical principles or religious rituals, but through the nitty-gritty realities of human history. "While the deities of other peoples were associated with places or things," writes Abraham Joshua Heschel, "the God of the prophets was the God of events: the Redeemer from slavery [and] the Revealer of the Torah."[3] The people of Israel honored God by marking time, stopping their ordinary activities for one day of the week. The Seder meal, the feasts of Tabernacles and Purim, all were re-enactments of events that had happened to their ancestors, taking place not somewhere up in the eternal realm between gods and demons, but in human space and time.

The Israelites also remembered God in stories. After they

2. Jacques Le Goff, *History and Memory*, trans. Steven Rendall and Elizabeth Claman (New York: Columbia University Press, 1992), pp. 68-71.

3. Abraham Joshua Heschel, *God in Search of Man* (New York: Harper Torchbooks, 1955), p. 200. See also Miroslav Volf, *The End of Memory: Remembering Rightly in a Violent World* (Grand Rapids: Eerdmans, 2006), pp. 96-102.

crossed the Jordan River into Canaan, ending forty years of wan-
dering in the wilderness, the first task was to erect a memorial in
the middle of the water. This mound of rocks piled one on the other
was not some mysterious symbol but meant to remind everyone of
a story: when the river stopped its flow while the Levites carried the
Ark of the Covenant into the land of promise. "In the future, when
your children ask you, 'What do these stones mean?'" Joshua ordered them, "tell them that the flow of the Jordan was cut off before
the ark of the covenant of the LORD." These stones, he said, "are to be
a memorial to the people of Israel forever" (Joshua 4:6-7).

The gospel accounts are similarly concerned with tracking
time. The life of Christ unfolds through festival seasons and har-
vests, cycles of life and death. But even more than that, we know
when Jesus came before Pilate — in the early morning — and the
exact time of his death — the "sixth hour," according to Luke. We
know that the resurrection took place in the wee hours of the first
day of the week. Why is all this detail necessary? Over and over the
gospel accounts reinforce what the Hebrew Scriptures had already
taught, that God dealt with creation according to the flow of the
human calendar. Jesus was a real person who lived on the earth
in what we have come to call the "first century." Moreover, like
the people of Israel, Christians also honor a "God of events." The
cycle of the liturgical year, beginning with Advent and continuing on through Christ's birth, death, resurrection and ascension
into heaven — followed by an interval of "ordinary time" — is not
a recital of magical or mythical episodes, but a way of keeping in
memory things that happened.

We have lost these rhythms. The modern view that history is
a luxury, a hobby for "buffs" and know-it-alls, puts us fundamentally out of step with all of our spiritual forebears. The past tense
is essential to our language of faith; without it our conversation is
limited and thin — and growing thinner all the time.

The Cost of Forgetting

In a broad sense we all believe that the past is important. Telling your life story to someone else cements a relationship more powerfully than all the flowers and candy in the world. As any therapist or doctor would say, talking through personal experiences is often the best way to unearth the "real me," that complicated person with a past carefully hidden from public view.

Moreover, most of us can also recite the famous line from the philosopher George Santayana that "those who forget the past are doomed to repeat it." When I used to ask college freshmen why they were required to take my class in World Civilization, they quickly zeroed in on this idea, that history is a tool for avoiding past mistakes. They also recognized that history can be inspirational, which is why we build monuments and museums and put up plaques and historical markers; we honor the Founding Fathers on the Fourth of July, soldiers on Veterans Day, and the Pilgrims on Thanksgiving.

But what do we *do* with those stories? It's hard to come up with any instances of our political leaders checking their history books before going to war, or deciding to include a historian or two in their circle of advisors. Learning from the past is a great idea that is almost never taken seriously. Certainly history can be inspirational, but once we have read the plaques and visited the monuments and watched the parades, then what? What exactly do old practices and beliefs — created by other people we will never know — have to do with the rigors of life in the twenty-first century?

These may seem like fairly abstract questions, but they are unavoidable and important ones. Sooner or later we will all have to deal with the past, usually when we are confronted with the endless dilemmas of keeping or tossing its physical "stuff." It might be an occasion as mundane as sorting through boxes for a yard sale, wondering what possessed us to buy an enormous stuffed animal or a pair of shoes two sizes too small. Or it will be as momentous as going through a parent's closets after the funeral, trying to decide what should be a keepsake and what should be thrown away.

The problem is equally if not more complex for local churches. At the Congregational Library we regularly field calls from church administrators wondering what to do with the piles of old ledgers and canceled checks that seem to have been growing since the Ice Age. Somehow it doesn't seem right to throw them away, but it doesn't make much sense to keep them around, either. Many churches, in fact, have records dating back centuries – to the point where those have become important historical artifacts – but they are hardly necessary for current church business. Mostly they take up space in a file cabinet, or are left in the care of someone drafted to be the "church historian."

For some congregations, the matter of keeping and tossing involves significant financial risk. Many older churches are the unintentional curators of valuable antiques, everything from eighteenth-century communion silver to ancient records and valuable paintings. Even the cost of insuring these objects is beyond most church budgets. Many churches are also saddled with the upkeep of beautifully historic – and frighteningly expensive – old buildings. When the steeple starts to lean or the nineteenth-century shingles begin to rot, the question naturally arises: what exactly is our debt to the past? Why not sell the communion silver to a collector and add a day care center? Somehow it might be a lot more practical to tear down the old building, designed for people with strong backs and long attention spans, and replace it with something new and far more ergonomic.

Of course, in other situations the past is not just irrelevant, it seems completely invisible. On one of my church visits to the Pacific Northwest the members told me with some chagrin that they didn't "have much history." I didn't agree with them but I knew what they meant. They didn't have an old building or a long line of retired pastors, much less eighteenth-century communion silver or tricorne hats in Plexiglas cases. Their buildings are no older than the suburban developments surrounding them, and the church's history falls within the living memory of older members.

Many congregations today were also born independent, organized without any direct connection to a historic denominational tradition. They are not Catholic or Protestant, Baptist or Presbyterian — they are simply Christian. The American landscape is full of these brand-new church congregations, built for people yearning for connection but wary of religious traditionalism. More and more, even denominational churches are adopting generic names that orient them to the present rather than the past. In theory at least, a "Community Fellowship" or the Church of the Bubbling Brook has no burden of history.

All of us, however, have a past. Even a sparkling new church plant in a west-coast suburb sits on thousands of years of time — the native and Spanish settlements established long before Plymouth Rock was a twinkle in a Pilgrim's eye. It also has a connection to the past in a larger sense. Whether we recognize it or not, we are part of the great — and sometimes not so great — tradition of the Christian church. We are all part of a network of belief going back two thousand years and encompassing millions of other people. When twenty-first-century Christians gather to sing and pray, when they practice the sacraments of baptism and communion, they are not making up those forms on the spot. All of those are an inheritance from centuries of Christian belief and practice.

So much has been forgotten. Few of us have had the opportunity to learn the long story of Christianity or of our own traditions in much depth, and the question is rarely addressed in religious education classes or from the pulpit. As a result, many Presbyterians and Baptists and Methodists can boast deep chronological roots but they have a shallow grasp of what those proper nouns really entail. The worship service can end up a hodgepodge of practices that may or may not have anything to do with any particular historical or theological tradition. Baptist confirmation classes kneel for a blessing and Congregational churches recite liturgies in naves with split chancels and stone altars against the back wall — seemingly unaware that many of their ancestors endured exile and death for opposing these very same practices.

When we do appropriate history we do it selectively, in bits and pieces deemed useful to life in the present. Thus the Founding Fathers speak to the issue of gay marriage and the Boston Tea Party provides a model for a twenty-first-century anti-tax movement. Alexander Hamilton, the "father of modern banking," advertises low interest rates, and Puritan rebel Anne Hutchinson is praised as the first American feminist. In church circles we want our history to be relevant and practical as well. We love lists of "famous firsts," special events or unusual people that demonstrate to the world our rock-solid orthodoxy or our progressive spirit (depending on the case).

This is not necessarily a bad thing — anything that makes the past compelling is an automatic plus — but it is selling history woefully short. We can stack up the heroes and heroines of the faith like a collection of baseball trading cards, but this does not mean we are taking the past seriously, much less seeing it through the lens of faith. In this book we will talk about a view of the past that is as rooted in Christian understanding as our view of the present should be. Instead of defining ourselves through associations with once-famous people, or taking our ancestors too lightly by assuming they were not as complex as we are, we should want an encounter with the past that will challenge and deepen our faith. What could be more practical than that?

Faith and History

In some ways, of course, history has become more popular among Christians than ever. Visit any religious bookstore, turn on cable television, or attend a public school committee hearing and the fact is unmistakable: the faith of the Founding Fathers is a hot topic. So is the Constitution and the Bill of Rights: many bestselling books – and not a few school textbooks – have sprung from arguments over whether the United States was established as a Christian nation.

Bestseller or not, this book takes a different path. Rather than debate the correct interpretation of the past, I am interested in the idea of the past itself. The real issue is not the particular stories we tell about George Washington kneeling to pray at Valley Forge or the Constitutional Convention establishing one nation under God, but why we believe that they matter in the first place.

And so most of this book has to do with the present. The opening three chapters describe different ways in which the modern world has shaped our view of historical events and people, and why it has become so difficult for us to feel a genuine connection with them. This is a huge issue, and for clarity's sake we will focus on three basic cultural assumptions: 1) that the past is "behind" us, 2) that it is inferior to the present, and 3) that it is not really real.

In the pages ahead we will take on some challenging ideas involving the broad and complex changes in the way western people think about time and human memory,[4] meet a few philosophers

4. Just a brief explanation: many of the examples in the next three chapters are taken from a relatively recent period in world history, the late nineteenth and early twentieth centuries. This period is not a turning point as much as a culmination of many changes taking place over long periods of time primarily within the western world, Europe and North America – and one I am particularly interested in as a historian.

and social theorists along the way, and work through some fairly abstract concepts. But the goal is simple: to help situate ourselves within the larger story of western culture and how it came to be "modern." The aim is to create critical distance toward our twenty-first-century world, and in that space to reconsider what it means to be part of the long Christian tradition. That means we will deal with everything from amusement parks and historical novels to Pilgrims, Catholic saints, and college freshmen. And though the topic is the meaning of the past, we are really working toward a richer, more complex understanding of our own time and place, toward a wiser way of being modern Christian people.

The next set of chapters, four and five, deal with the significance of religious traditions and the relationship between the living and the dead. Both have deep roots in Christian history, and are basic to any recovery of memory in our time. They also shift our gaze outward, helping us to see ourselves as integral parts of a very long story with more subplots and a larger cast of characters than we can begin to imagine.

The title of this book suggests that remembering can become a spiritual practice, and this is the subject that the last chapter tackles in some depth. This does not mean that the study of history should become a devotional exercise in which God is dragged into every plot twist and the moral lesson comes tied up in a bow. Understanding human history can take a lot of intellectual elbow grease, and a commitment to reading and learning and analyzing. Moreover, the spiritual practice of remembering is more fundamental than mining the experiences of others for our individual spiritual benefit, though that is certainly possible. It is another way of understanding the world and our place in it, as we move through time as well as space. It means opening ourselves to a different way of seeing all the many ways our lives connect to those of others — past, present, and future.

CHAPTER ONE

Stranded in the Present

In the endless war for ratings and viewers, a local news station I once knew decided to air the late edition an hour earlier than its competitors. "At ten it's news," the announcer would solemnly intone, "and at eleven it's history."

That tagline used to irritate me no end. The worst part was the confident assumption that the present is all we need to worry about, and that anything before is automatically stale and irrelevant. History is literally yesterday's news.[1]

Prejudice against the past runs deep in American culture, and it comes in many forms: declining enrollments in history classes, the thoughtless destruction of old historic buildings, and the endless race for the new and improved. Even basic knowledge about when the Civil War took place or the connection between Martin Luther and the Reformation seems to be dying away. As a former history teacher, I will not easily forget final examinations insisting that "when Abraham Lincoln became president, all the colonies rejoiced," or that the Chinese practiced a philosophy of "confusionism."

Yet even the worst curmudgeon would have to admit that in

---

1. The title for this chapter is taken from Peter Fritzsche, *Stranded in the Present: Modern Time and the Melancholy of History* (Cambridge: Harvard University Press, 2004).

a thousand other ways Americans remain absolutely enamored with history. On cable television the History Channel offers an endless store of World War II footage; bestseller lists regularly feature biographies of historical figures like John Adams, Benjamin Franklin, and Harry Truman. People still flock to sites like Colonial Williamsburg and Plimoth Plantation, to old forts and sailing ships and train museums. Thousands of re-enactors stage and re-stage the great battles of American history, from the Revolutionary War to Viet Nam, all in painstaking historical detail.

A quick visit to the Internet will likewise confirm that we are a culture obsessed with memory keeping — with archiving, documenting, or digitizing seemingly anything that falls in the path of a camera lens. Historical documents scholars once traveled thousands of miles to see are now available on their computer screens, and in many cases adapted for easy electronic searching. What once took weeks of reading through ancient handwriting and hoping for mention of a particular name or event now takes minutes. If anything, one observer has argued, we suffer from a "hypertrophy" of memory; we want to hold on to old things long after we have forgotten the stories that give them meaning.[2]

Zeal for preservation has become one of our distinguishing features. Certainly honoring the past is nothing new in human history, but as historian David Lowenthal points out, traveling collections usually featured objects that were unique and significant. People went to see the oddities in a P. T. Barnum circus or curiosities brought back by explorers at the risk of life and limb. The rarer the object and the harder to retrieve, the more it deserved to be displayed and treasured. Now our collecting is almost indiscriminate. We have museums dedicated to everything from the history

2. Quoted in Bradford Vivian, *Public Forgetting: The Rhetoric and Politics of Beginning Again* (University Park: Pennsylvania State University Press, 2010), p. 4.

of string to World War II airplanes, from dolls and Tupperware to arrowheads and baseball cards. No one loves a display of antique lunchboxes better than I do, but the fact that someone has gone to the trouble to assemble all of them raises some questions. In fact, Lowenthal cites a figure that 95 percent of all the museums today were built in the second half of the twentieth century. "Never before," writes Lowenthal, "have so many been so engaged with so many different pasts." We seem almost terrified of forgetting anything.[3]

Why such extremes? Though critics may complain loud and often about historical illiteracy and the sloppy reading habits of the general public, at bottom the issue is not more and better books. It is not about bulking up the high school history curricula or more field trips to museums. In fact, all the finger-wagging in the world will not change anything: the reasons behind our "memory problem" are long in the making and they are woven deeply into modern culture.

The place to begin, then, is understanding what we mean when we say we live in a "modern" world. Without a doubt life is different from what it was even a century ago; we can point to any number of inventions and conveniences which shape our daily routines in ways that our grandparents could not have imagined. But these outward changes are just the tip of the proverbial iceberg. More important still are the ways we have come to think about the world, other people, and ourselves.

These changes took place across a long period of time in the western world – and here we mean Europe and North America primarily. Historians may debate when or where or how "modernity" began – this is what they do of course – but in general we can

3. David Lowenthal, *Possessed by the Past: The Heritage Crusade and the Spoils of History* (New York: Free Press, 1996), pp. 3, 5.

say that we are dealing with a fairly large chunk of time, rooted somewhere in the eighteenth-century "Age of Reason." But the exact timeframe and mechanics are not the issue here; what's more important is a subtle, large-scale cultural shift that has shaped our sense of memory today, as well as the way people have learned to measure and see themselves in time.

Being Modern

In a general sense, modern means "new," the eternal search for anything that is faster, bigger, or better than the old. But it also means something more. The word itself dates back to the fifth century, when people were searching for a way to describe the collapse of the Roman Empire, an epic event that shook their sense of historical continuity. For most of human history, people had assumed that the past was the pattern for the present – the absolutely new and completely unprecedented was in a very basic way just not possible. *Moderna* was a word that referred to the destruction of something old and the start of something new – an end that brought forth another beginning. The idea attached to that word has persisted: to be modern is to make a complete break with the past.

Over time, the word took on different shades of meaning but kept that ambiguous sense of loss and discovery. We can imagine that for many people modernity was cause for mourning, the end of treasured folkways; for others the past was little more than the dead weight of tradition, and always better gone. In our own time the second meaning has won out: the new sets the agenda for the old, and has become increasingly more important and desirable. Better to have the latest in automobile technology than to face the horror of driving around in "your father's Oldsmobile." Better to discard last year's pastel socks or platform shoes than to risk ending up on someone's worst-dressed list. As Karl Marx once said, the modern world is one in which "all that is solid melts into air."

In a deeper sense, then, modernity is a "permanent present," as one historian has described it.[4] In many parts of the world we can look around and see this to be true in the newness of the landscape. Anything older than fifty years has simply disappeared, destroyed by the twentieth century's terrible history of wars and genocide. Over several decades we have seen the great castles and cathedrals of Europe, the temples and monuments of Asia, and the ancient treasures of the Euphrates River Valley pummeled into dust with no hope of resurrection. By the irony of war some of our most ancient cities — Nagasaki, London, and Hamburg — appear to be the newest.

In a less dramatic fashion, forgetting has become part of daily life for millions of people in cities and suburbs around the world. As I look out my office window I see buildings that were not there two years ago, and watch people walk by with new gadgets I despair of ever mastering. The city skyline is forever rising and falling, clothing styles change from year to year, and computer technology veers from one new achievement to another. We would be silly to be nostalgic for a clunky wireless phone from the 1970s, or the office furniture the company replaced last month.

This is "how modernity forgets," as social theorist Paul Connerton has argued. People who regularly see buildings and streets torn down to make way for something else end up with a particular view of the world. "Things" carry less meaning for them. They do not form deep attachments to a comb or an office desk or a skyscraper, not just because these are replaceable but because no one

---

4. The phrase is from Eric Hobsbawm, *The Age of Extremes: The History of the World, 1914-1991* (New York: Vintage Books, 1994), p. 3.

really knows where they came from. In a sense, these are objects without a past. We know nothing of the time and the labor, much less the people, involved in building our brand-new condominium or the clothes we bought at the local shopping mall. We did not see the local grocery store grow from an idea to a set of design plans to a schedule for construction. It is simply there.[5]

Centuries ago, however, people could walk by a house or a church or a fort and know who built it and something of the struggle and difficulties it took to finish. They might well know the family living there, going back many generations; they would be able to talk about the woods or the swamp that had been there before, and who first cleared the land or laid the first foundation. Those buildings all had human stories behind them; in other words, they had a *history*.

Now, in a world without these memories, anything is possible. In my own city of Boston a developer has recently purchased the old Charles Street Jail and turned it into a high-priced hotel and restaurant. For many years this grim granite building was home to the city's most wretched and desperate citizens. Malcolm X began his conversion to Islam within its walls, and in the 1920s the Italian anarchists Sacco and Vanzetti stayed there awaiting trial. Even one of the mayors of Boston, James Michael Curley, did time at the Charles Street Jail, in his case for helping out a friend by taking a civil service examination for him. The developer, in a lighthearted nod to the past, decided to name it the "Liberty Hotel" and kept the old catwalks as design motifs around the central atrium. The hotel restaurant was named "The Clink," incorporating former jail cells, complete with barred doors, into cozy booths for quiet dining. All this is possible because the jail's

5. Paul Connerton, *How Modernity Forgets* (Cambridge: Cambridge University Press, 2009), pp. 51, 52, 53.

violent and painful history has been forgotten, tastefully remodeled into a building without a past.

The Rules

One of the most treasured beliefs of our age is that we are free to express ourselves in unique and individual ways. Sons are no longer required to follow their fathers' trade, and daughters do not have to confine themselves to the kitchen and the nursery. We raise our children to be adventurous and independent and innovative.

In many ways, however, we are far less free than our ancestors. We live according to the "rules" of modern culture, within a kind of bargain that allows us freedom of expression but also imposes limits on us. Examples are everywhere: in order to get the wonderful technology that brings the world of social networking into a personal phone, people will endure hours of sales pitches, long waits on hold, and an ever-growing list of mysterious costs. Freedom, as it turns out, is expensive and time-consuming.

My favorite example of this paradox is the amusement park. These sprang up about a century ago as a way for overworked city people to blow off some steam and have some innocent fun. But it was a kind of fun different from anything the world had seen – in an amusement park everyone enjoyed the same thing at the same time and in the same way. New York's famous Coney Island park began as a seaside retreat, a place where an adventurous few began to wear scandalous "bathing costumes" – and in mixed company, no less. Old photographs of the beach show the silly meandering play of people on a day off, striking odd poses and mugging for the camera. Contrast this to the endlessly repeatable fun of a roller coaster or a Ferris wheel, dispensing thrills with mechanical precision for hours, days, and years on end. While the size and scale of the amusement park promised endless pleasure, the fun was anything but spontaneous. Modern individualism comes with rules and limits.[6]

This does not mean that amusement parks are intrinsically evil (with the possible exception of Disney World); they are simply one example of a larger reality we take for granted all the time. Our freedom of expression has grown in tandem — and sometimes in tension — with a world that is becoming always more ordered and predictable. This not a sinister plot or a paranoid fantasy; both freedom and order have their benefits. Nor is it something we can alter in any way; it is woven into the logic of the modern world. Even our hipsters and individualists seem to rebel in surprisingly similar ways, following a dress code as intricate as any Wall Street banker, down to the style of hair, boots and glasses, piercings and tattoos.

Philosopher Charles Taylor describes the changes taking place across the last several centuries as a shift from a "boundless" universe to a "bounded" one. Ironically, it is not the pre-modern world that is surrounded by limits, but our modern one. In the boundless world, before the eighteenth-century Age of Reason, people assumed that angels, demons, and saints lived among them. They inhabited in a world open to supernatural happenings — miraculous cures or divine visitations, for example — since there was no metaphysical roof separating them from the powerful invisible beings hovering above and around them. We could call their world "enchanted," in the sense that the unusual and unexplainable were always possible. A saint could suddenly appear in a tree or a grotto; a piece of the true Cross could cure illnesses and ward off evil.

But this porous universe was also unpredictable. Long-term planning was pointless with the constant threat of interruption by

6. John Kasson, *Amusing the Million: Coney Island at the Turn of the Century* (New York: Hill and Wang, 1978), pp. 82, 105.

sudden supernatural events or malevolent forces. Though we may enjoy a film about monsters and lightheartedly dress up as witches and ghosts at Halloween, our ancestors, says Taylor, "would have found this incomprehensible." These beings were not only real but terribly dangerous.[7]

Our world today is bounded. One major part of the change from the rural and slow-moving world of the past to the efficient urban and industrial one of today is the elimination of random intrusions by ghosts and spirits. Our world is buffered from outside transcendent forces, and because of that we are not afraid to plan for the future. There is little point in weighing other alternatives: what we might have lost in wonder, we have gained in security. Our world is more controlled and predictable in ways that the old one was not, and we can see meaning and purpose in our actions.

Religion still exists in this world, and in many ways vigorously so, but within a much narrower framework. From a society "in which it was virtually impossible not to believe in God," says Taylor, we now live in one "in which faith, even for the staunchest believer, is one human possibility among others." Belief, in other words, is a personal option, selected according to need and taste. But all of us, believers and nonbelievers alike, live behind the same protected shield, and have accepted the benefits and the losses of a bounded world.[8]

Being modern is complicated. Our lives are a mixture of open-ended freedom – the kind that lets us flout convention and pursue individual tastes and preferences – and deeply rooted control. Western-style modernity offers us free play for the imagination,

7. Charles Taylor, "Western Secularity," in *Rethinking Secularism*, ed. Craig Calhoun, Mark Juergensmeyer, and Jonathan VanAntwerpen (New York: Oxford University Press, 2011), p. 39.

8. Charles Taylor, *A Secular Age* (Cambridge, Mass.: Harvard University Press, 2007); Taylor, "Western Secularity," p. 42.

but within an ever-growing framework of order. It is both a gain and a loss.

Modern Time

The idea of boundedness helps us grasp what it means to be "stranded in the present." Just as we assume certain things about the relationship between the seen and unseen world, we harbor assumptions about the relationship between the past, present, and future, and about the meaning of time itself. Here we could easily wander into a forest of abstractions about time and eternity, being and nothingness, and so on — but that is not our destination, and I would get us lost fairly quickly. The best way to understand the way modernity works is to start with the pre-modern world, before people learned to measure their days around clocks and Daylight Savings Time, or to divide their days and nights into boxes on a page and segments on a line.

In this unbounded western world, time was fluid and unpredictable. Historians tell us that in the medieval era, no one expected it to be moving constantly forward. People allowed for oscillations and jumps, moments when the world of eternity and the realm of human beings suddenly overlapped. Time was "layered on various tracks," Carlos Eire explains in his wonderful book *A Very Brief History of Eternity*. It was "studded with vertical doorways" and thresholds that opened to wonders on special days in the liturgical calendar. On days honoring saints or remembering the birth and death of Jesus, "one could find oneself transported to higher realities and eternal moments, if one paid attention."[9]

9. Carlos Eire, *A Very Brief History of Eternity* (Princeton: Princeton and Oxford University Presses, 2010), p. 92.

In fact the word *secular* originally referred to people living outside the regular cycles of liturgical time. The so-called secular clergy were parish priests who lived outside of monasteries; in contrast to the cloistered clergy who followed the daily rhythms of matins and vespers, these men preached and taught and worked within the rules set by the temporal world and its own rhythms of market days and the planting and harvesting of crops.

The Christian liturgical calendar still captures this sense of oscillation between higher and ordinary time. In contrast to what social theorist Walter Benjamin has described as the "homogeneous, empty time" of modernity, the church year moves through the story of Christ's birth, death, and resurrection in a constantly repeating cycle of life and death, hope and sadness, allowing believers to be spiritually present in all those biblical events. In a sense, time is vertical rather than horizontal — as Taylor explains, "this year's Good Friday can be closer to the Crucifixion than [it is to] last year's mid-summer day."[10]

This explains why a medieval painting can show a twelfth-century nobleman in his best suit of clothes gathered around the cradle of the baby Jesus with a troop of first-century shepherds. People of the medieval world, writes historian Jacques Le Goff, lived "in a constant anachronism," "tossed back and forth between the past and the future." There was no reason why Mary and Jesus could not pose in medieval dress in front of a castle window, or the flight to Egypt take the Holy Family past a European village covered in snow. Time was not relentlessly chronological.[11]

Since then, all of western culture — and more and more of the rest of the world — has adopted the strict and increasingly un-

10. Walter Benjamin, *Illuminations* (London: Fontana, 1973), p. 263, quoted in Taylor, *A Secular Age*, pp. 45-61.

11. Jacques Le Goff, *History and Memory* trans. Steven Rendall and Elizabeth Claman (New York: Columbia University Press, 1992), p. 13.

breakable rules of secular time. From the invention of the pendulum clock in 1657 to the introduction of World Standard Time in 1884, western people have learned to accept ever more precise, abstract, and overarching principles of timekeeping.[12] We do not set our clocks randomly according to what is most convenient, nor do we show up for an appointment when the mood strikes, or when we feel on a *personal* level that it is four o'clock in the afternoon. We understand, first of all, that time is uniform; it proceeds at the same pace and in the same ordered segments in every place across the world.

If time can be measured, it can also be bought and sold. In the early nineteenth century, when mills and factories began paying workers by the hour, many people found the idea absolutely horrifying. What incentive would a worker have if every minute brought the same compensation as the one before? What would happen to the work ethic if everyone were paid the same amount? When nearly everyone lived on farms, as most Americans did well into the twentieth century, work was never this uniform. During spring planting or the fall harvest the days were long and exhausting, but in the winter there was relatively little to do besides wait for spring. Moreover, the wage for farm work was not money but food to eat, with perhaps some left over to sell or barter, while factory workers took home nothing but the money they were paid for their labor. They worked the same hours at the same pace regardless of the time of year or the number of bills to pay.

We are now so used to talking about time in economic metaphors that we barely notice. But they are everywhere. Smart, forward-looking people *save* time but foolish people *lose* it. The unmotivated *waste* their days doing nothing, while others *invest*

12. Lynn Hunt, *Measuring Time, Making History* (Budapest and New York: Central European University Press, 2008), p. 10.

them wisely in a worthwhile project. People can *take up* our time, or *give* us some of theirs. Not all time is worth the same, either. By the rules of the marketplace, a CEO's time is worth far more than a teacher's — or a historian's.

One last characteristic of modern time bears noting: we believe not only that it is moving, but also that it is moving *forward*. In other words, the future always lies ahead, and the past always behind us. We also believe that time moves forward in a variety of different ways. Historians talk about turning points, rises and declines, and periods of intense and less intense change — all part of the "time map" modern western people carry in their heads. This may seem just a matter of common sense, but it is hardly universal. Some South American tribespeople point ahead of themselves instead of behind when talking about the past. Other cultures have calendars without any regularly repeating patterns at all, no neat solid blocks of weeks and months and years; time comes in clusters of days that begin and end according to the say-so of tribal leaders. In every culture, the ways we measure time and the ways we experience it are different, built to reflect our beliefs and values.[13]

The idea of time as a forward-moving line is a hallmark of western culture, deeply woven into the ways we think about everything, from biological evolution to the narratives of our lives as we pass from childhood to old age. This is different from the idea that things change or even the belief that time has a direction. From Augustine on down through prophecy bestsellers like *The Late Great Planet Earth*, Christians have understood that God works out divine purposes within human history, sometimes in painful ways and sometimes in blessed ones. At times the trajectory is downward, when evil threatens to overcome good; but in

---

13. Eva Hoffman, *Time* (New York: Picador, 2009), pp. 119-31; Eviatar Zerubavel, *Time Maps: Collective Memory and the Social Shape of the Past* (Chicago: University of Chicago Press, 2003).

the end God always metes out justice, and the ultimate triumph of love and peace seems close to hand. What is new and different in modern thinking is the assumption that change means progress. Forward motion is always upward motion – hence the notion that we "stand on the shoulders" of our ancestors, or that we have a higher vantage point and better light than those trapped in the dark recesses of the past.

By definition modern time is inexorable, as ordered and controlled as the mechanical fun of an amusement park. This does not mean our sense of time is intrinsically evil: imagine city life if everyone ignored the clock and worked according to personal needs and preferences. Life is infinitely better when trains run on time. But if we step back from the practicalities, we can see what has been lost in the process. If time is always moving forward, the past is always becoming more distant and more irrelevant. In a sense, modern people are "stranded in the present," without a meaningful connection to anything that has gone before.[14]

And so we visit the past as tourists. Sometimes this is literally so, when we take in Colonial Williamsburg and Plimoth Plantation, or travel around to Civil War battlefields. But it is also true in a metaphorical sense. The past has become a strange and distant country, full of odd people and mysterious customs. And though seeing how these people built their homes or raised their children can broaden the mind, most of us don't go back home determined to learn how to use an axe or a hickory stick. Knowledge about those strange customs might be interesting, but it is not essential – it does not change our way of doing things. In the end we will always prefer our own land in the present. At the end of the tour there is an air-conditioned car and a comfortable hotel room waiting, complete with cable television and refrigerated food.

14. Fritzsche, *Stranded in the Present*, pp. 5, 54.

There is nothing intrinsically wrong with enjoying the past this way – it can be a lot of fun, in fact. But it could be so much more. The thousands of people who visit Boston and have only a few days to walk the Freedom Trail, visit Fenway Park, and eat a lobster dinner cannot even scratch the surface of what the city is really like. They have not inhaled the comforting mixture of exhaust fumes and roasted cashews that hangs in the city subways on humid summer days, or learned to love the particular slant of the New England sun on a winter afternoon.

The same would be true of a Bostonian on a day trip to Chicago, Tokyo, Budapest, or Khartoum. The visit would be exciting, but would not make them cosmopolitan. Becoming something more than a casual time-tourist requires a willingness to be challenged and changed, just as living in India or Ghana or Peru will upend any American's assumptions about money and wealth.

Yearning

When I was ten, I had two great wishes. Every time I found a four-leaf clover or split a wishbone I wished first for a horse and then for a time machine. Although I had never taken riding lessons, I spent hours daydreaming about turning our suburban garage into a stall and tack room and our backyard into a paddock, picturing my horse and me trotting around leafy cul-de-sacs and leaping over picket fences. I was also passionate about the Revolutionary War. I knew far too much for a girl my age about eighteenth-century battles and ships and cannons, having pored over the World Book Encyclopedia entry for the "American Revolution," and read every book on the subject in our tiny school library at least twice. I simply yearned to be alive in 1776. For reasons now obvious, rebels like Samuel Adams, Paul Revere, and Patrick Henry – he was the one who insisted on "liberty or death" — had a powerful hold on someone leaving childhood in the mid-1960s.

Becoming an adult meant that I gave up on the garage-stable idea, and it also meant that I began to understand how time worked. Like all of us, I came to the terrible realization that I was going to die. The days behind me were not just over, but forever gone. The past and the person I used to be had vanished; they could not be fixed or altered, much less visited. In fact, if I had a time machine today, I would probably skip the glory days of 1776 and go back to the magical time when I was ten.

This fixed gulf between past and present is central to what it means to be modern, to live in the future tense. Certainly we still yearn for the past; in fact the current passion for history is to a large degree a way of staving off a sense of loneliness. The objects we keep, says David Lowenthal, are "remnants of stability," "islands of security in seas of change."[15]

In other words, we are nostalgic. That English word is a combination of two Greek ones: *nostos* for "return" and *algos* for "suffering." It describes the fate of the fabled Odysseus, who so famously endured the pain of being stranded far from home. Yet as novelist Milan Kundera points out, the terrible ache is not just about the miles between you and your loved ones. In Portuguese, for example, the word for nostalgia is *saudade*. The translation is not completely accurate because it includes two separate kinds of loss, the pain of separation from home and the fear of forgetting the people and places that used to be familiar and important. When we say we are nostalgic, Kundera implies, we are expressing the pain of homesickness for a place to which we can no longer return — and one we can no longer remember.[16]

15. Lowenthal, *Possessed by the Past*, p. 7.
16. Milan Kundera, *Ignorance*, trans. Linda Asher (New York: HarperCollins, 2006), pp. 5, 6.

All of this makes liturgical time that much more important to recovery of those memories. Observing the church's calendar year — the one that begins with Advent and continues on through Epiphany, Lent, Easter, and Pentecost and then into "ordinary time" — is not just an interesting thing to do; it could possibly save our souls. Most of us have never experienced the reality of night without an electric outlet or neon sign. We can shop for groceries or fill up with gas any time within the twenty-four-hour cycle, even on Christmas and Thanksgiving. Thanks to the proliferation of electronic gadgets, fewer of us are enjoying the weekend break from work and the nagging demands of our email. Liturgical time, as we have seen, rests on an older chronological sense, one that goes back before the unbreakable regimens of our days. And so the simple act of keeping Sabbath, of refusing to give in to the inexorable flow of modern time and keeping a separate rhythm of darkness and light, joy and repentance, is profoundly counter-cultural. We do not celebrate Christmas from the day after Thanksgiving to December 26 — we live in holy expectation during the four weeks of Advent. We do not march into church on Easter Sunday all dressed up to celebrate, but experience this day as the culmination of seven weeks of penitence and reflection during Lent.

All of this means that we can "inhabit the present with a certain lightness of being." That is not permission to ignore modern time or to set ourselves apart in holy sanctimony; it means recognizing that in a sense we are "strangers and pilgrims in a foreign territory," grounded in the past and yearning for the future fulfillment of God's kingdom.[17] Our real rhythm of time originates not from Greenwich, England, or the moon or the sun, but from a person, Jesus Christ, whose short human life (of some thirty-three

17. James K. A. Smith, *Desiring the Kingdom: Worship, Worldview, and Cultural Formation* (Grand Rapids: Baker Academic, 2009), p. 157.

years) and eternal living presence forever altered the days, weeks, years, and millennia of western time. Ours, says mystical writer Evelyn Underhill, is the "leisure of Eternity."[18]

18. Evelyn Underhill, *The Spiritual Life* (New York: Harper, 1937), p. 98.

CHAPTER TWO

Past Imperfect

Robert Elsmere is the story of a young English minister who lost his faith. Published in Great Britain in 1888, the novel clearly touched a spiritual nerve, selling over a million copies on both sides of the Atlantic. Mary Augusta Ward, the author, knew the religious struggles of her time firsthand. Her uncle was Matthew Arnold, whose poem "Dover Beach" remains one of the most eloquent expressions of spiritual doubt, and her nephew was Aldous Huxley, author of the novel *Brave New World*.

As Robert Elsmere's story opens, our hero is newly married and intellectually hungry, but he is trapped by the endless needs of his poverty-ridden parish. Against his better judgment he strikes up a relationship with the local squire, Robert Wendover. Though Wendover's selfishness is one of the main causes for the suffering of Elsmere's parishioners, the two men share a love of books, and warily at first, they begin to read and talk together.

The squire's library is full of radical atheist literature, but none of it plants the fatal seed of doubt in the young minister's heart. In the end, it is not a failed argument for God's existence or discovery of errors in the Bible that brings about his downfall. Robert Elsmere's slide to unbelief begins while he is reading a history of France.

At first, the earnest young pastor is completely absorbed in

31

the account, devouring tales about ancient French kings and peasants with "imagination and sympathy." Their stories give him a "passionate sense of the human problems" underlying the dry and dusty details of history, especially as the sufferings of the poor in eighteenth-century France resonate with those of his struggling parishioners in modern-day England. This kind of encounter with the past is downright exhilarating, giving Elsmere a sense of connection to thousands of people he will never have the chance to meet.

But his new circle of worldly friends is not impressed. They begin to challenge him with questions that seem arcane and abstract at first, but soon lead the naïve young man onto dangerous ground. In the roundabout way so characteristic of nineteenth-century novels, one of them asks, " '[D]id the man of the third century understand, or report, or interpret facts in the same way as the man of the sixteenth or the nineteenth?' " " 'And if not,' " his friend presses further, " 'what are the differences, and what are the deductions to be made from them, if any?' " To translate: how can you assume that you and anyone from the past are seeing the world the same way?

At this moment, the foundations of Elsmere's faith begin to crumble. Once he was an enthusiastic amateur historian, living happily among his ancestors, whom he considered "bone of his bone, flesh of his flesh." But now they are changing before his eyes. The men and women of ancient France are becoming incomprehensible and foreign, figures in a "strange puppet-show." On one level they are utterly familiar — they are "kings, bishops, judges, poets, priests, [and] men of letters." But what a "gulf between him and them!" As a man of the late-nineteenth century, Elsmere has nothing more in common with these people than he might with a Bedouin herding sheep in the Sahara Desert. Here is the dawning truth: each period of time has its own set of rules "born with a man and tainting his whole ways of seeing and thinking from childhood to the grave!"[1]

Like any Victorian novel worth its salt, *Robert Elsmere* ends with a great deal of hand-wringing. Loss of certainty takes an enormous toll, destroying not just the young minister's Christian convictions but his physical and mental health. Although Elsmere spends the last several chapters of the novel busily engaged in doing good, trying to help the poor of London, this is only a partial consolation for his lost faith. His good works are a way of keeping those creeping questions about truth at bay, and in the end Elsmere simply dies of exhaustion, a noble but deeply disappointed man.

What do we make of this story? In some ways it is familiar and in others absolutely astonishing. Today, very few people lose their faith watching the History Channel or turn into atheists while they are strolling the grounds of Colonial Williamsburg. Why did the history of France destroy Robert Elsmere's faith in God?

This question is the subject of this chapter. We will be looking at another way of being modern, dealing not just with our sense of time but by our idea of the past itself. And this path, as the story of Robert Elsmere suggests, takes us directly into questions about faith and doubt, opening the possibility that history is no longer the ally of believers, but in fact a primary enemy.

The actual stories found in history books – the endless descriptions of religious wars and corrupt church leaders, murder and mayhem in the name of God – are not our primary problem. Although these kinds of things are depressing to read about, they should not be terribly startling to anyone who has lived through the past century. None of us should be surprised to see the people of God behaving badly.

1. Mary Augusta Ward, *Robert Elsmere* (New York and London: Macmillan and Co., 1888; reprint University of Nebraska, 1967), pp. 198, 199.

For most people the real nub of the problem is the foreignness of the past. It has become, as one author quipped, "a foreign country," a land of strange customs and exotic ideas.[2] And as it has become less familiar, it has also become more distant, more arcane, and less relevant. As Robert Elsmere realizes so painfully, the people of medieval France are not "bone of his bone and flesh of his flesh," but the mysterious creations of another time and place. They did not simply live earlier in time than Elsmere, but in a profoundly different political, religious, economic, and social context.

The idea that the past is not just "before" but "different" became a part of western thinking during that formative period we looked at in the previous chapter, when the western world shifted from a medieval outlook to a modern, secular one. For our purposes, the most important part of the shift was the simultaneous loss of the past and the emergence of a secular or "bounded" view of the world. This deep and important cultural change brings us closer to the heart of Elsmere's doubts, to understanding why his painful discovery about French peasants alienates him from God.

To understand what was going on, we need to deal with a set of ideas so taken for granted that we barely notice its presence any more. What we casually refer to as "historical perspective" is part of the air we breathe, an assumption so basic to our sense of the world and of ourselves that it becomes almost invisible – which is precisely why the idea needs a bit of unpacking.

2. This is the first line in L. P. Hartley's novel, *The Go-Between*, first published in 1953.

Napoleon in Flip-Flops

We have already seen in the previous chapter that pre-modern people had a different understanding of time. Rather than an eternally growing horizontal line, for them it was a single whole, one where people long dead – including saints and ghosts – still associated with the living. Certainly people carried memories of their lives and stories about their ancestors – they understood "before" and "after" – but they were not bound as we are to a strict sense of chronological time. In a way, there was no such thing as the past, at least in the way we conceive it, as something entirely separate from the present.

In other words, no one worried about anachronisms, the misplacing of people, events, or customs into the "wrong" time period. As we saw in the previous chapter, medieval paintings often mingled characters from Bible stories with German and Frankish kings and princes, peasants and soldiers. Roman soldiers marched around in European armor, while Aristotle and Plato strolled through Christian cathedrals wearing the gowns and caps of medieval scholars.

Today we have strict rules about this. Certain things belong in certain time periods and not in others. It is simply impossible to believe that an Egyptian Pharaoh would worry about his hairline and try to trim down his paunch the way modern men do; or that the emperor Napoleon would spend his days off in boxer shorts and a T-shirt, stretched out in his throne room with a beer and the latest news from the French fencing team. In fact, these kind of historical mistakes are good ways of getting us to laugh. Movies like "Monty Python and the Holy Grail" or even Mark Twain's novel *A Connecticut Yankee in King Arthur's Court* make endlessly clever use of anachronisms, from a medieval peasant heaving piles of mud and muttering about "anarcho-syndicalist radicalism" to Sir Lancelot riding a bicycle into battle.

This is because we understand the past as a distinct space, one that is "back there" in time and operating under its own set of rules. Napoleon lived in an age that demanded a more formal military wardrobe and had no notions of a day off; Pharaohs did not worry about their masculinity. We are all creatures of context, the product of "historical development amid ever-changing circumstances."[3]

There is more to the idea of historical perspective than just difference, however. We have also come to understand that everything around us, from politics and literature to art and architecture, is made by human beings for other human beings. "Historicism," as this notion is called, assumes that none of these landed on the earth from above, a set of ideas sealed off from every form of human contamination.

In one sense historicism is not a particularly difficult concept; unless we want to believe that everything in the world simply dropped from the sky, it just makes good sense. It helps us see how human beings have fashioned worlds that mirrored their understanding of the universe. It is a tool for understanding how cultures grow and develop, and how they are different from each other in ways both subtle and enormous.

In a larger sense, however, historicism has upended the world for people of faith. It is, as social theorist Ernst Troeltsch once observed, "a leaven that alters everything," from the most advanced academic study to the simplest expressions of faith. More than just a way of understanding the past, it has become one of the most difficult forms of modern skepticism, and one that is central to our present-day secular world.[4]

3. Zachary Sayre Schiffman, *The Birth of the Past* (Baltimore: The Johns Hopkins University Press, 2011), p. 273.

4. Troeltsch quoted in Thomas Howard, *Religion and the Rise of Historicism: W. M. L. DeWette, Jacob Burckhardt, and the Theological Origins of Nineteenth-*

Abraham the Chaldean

We can investigate this side of the problem with another late-nineteenth-century novel about a young minister's fall from grace. (Yes, Victorian readers had an endless fascination with misbehaving clergymen, both fictional and real.) *The Damnation of Theron Ware* was written by an American author, Harold Frederic, and it was an instant success when it was published in 1896. Like Robert Elsmere, Theron Ware is a sincere but restless pastor, trapped in a small-town Methodist church full of small-minded parishioners. He decides to supplement his meager salary by writing a popular book on the life of Abraham, the Old Testament patriarch. What could possibly go wrong? Here was a dramatic tale of a son rebelling against the evil ways of his idol-worshipping family; the more he thinks about it, the more Theron becomes convinced that "the hand of Providence" is behind his choice. "The book was to be blessed from its very inception."

But Ware's confidence does not last long. The more he works on the book, the more he begins to realize the depth of his ignorance about history — no thanks to his library of pious literature published by the Methodist Book Concern. So Theron decides to read through Abraham's story in the opening chapters of Genesis on his own. He has preached from these texts many times and they are utterly familiar — but this time, all of a sudden, something shifts. The "halo of sanctification" around Abraham and his family drops away, and Ware sees them for the first time as "untutored and unwashed barbarians, filled with animal lusts and ferocities, struggling by violence and foul chicanery to secure a foothold in a country which did not belong to them, — all rude tramps and rob-

---

Century Historical Consciousness (Cambridge: Cambridge University Press, 2000), p. 16.

bers of the uncivilized plain." Maybe Theron's book project wasn't such a great idea after all. From Abraham's sneaky and lustful nephew Lot to his own quarreling and violent grandsons, the stories of Genesis are hardly decent fare for God-fearing Methodists.

But the worst realization is still to come. Suddenly it dawns on Theron Ware that Abraham was a "Chaldean." To him, at this moment, this is a terribly uncomfortable idea, throwing his stomach into knots. No more the white-bearded grandfather of nineteenth-century Sunday school books, Abraham was someone who grew up in an ancient Mediterranean culture, an alien figure from a bloodthirsty time and place. The Abraham of the Methodist Book Concern looked like he could understand, and maybe even help with, the concerns of Theron Ware's congregation. The Chaldean Abraham emphatically did not care.

To make matters worse, the novel provides Theron Ware with a new set of jaded freethinking friends every bit as insidious as Robert Elsmere's. When Ware begins to talk, timidly at first, about his research on Abraham, one of them gently scolds him. "I fear that you are taking our friend Abraham too literally, Mr. Ware," the tempter chides. "Modern research, you know, quite wipes him out of existence as an individual. The word 'Abram' is merely an eponym, – it means 'exalted father.'" In fact, Ware's friend declares, "Abraham is not a person at all: he is a tribe, a sept, a clan."[5]

Robert Elsmere only had to deal with French peasants; Theron Ware's problem with history involved the sacred words of Scripture. The conversation about Abraham launches into an extended explanation of Hebrew names, and ends with a casual reference to "this Christ-myth of ours." By then Theron Ware is thoroughly

5. Harold Frederic, *The Damnation of Theron Ware* (1896; reprint New York: Holt, Rinehart and Winston, Inc., 1960), pp. 39-40, 61-62, 69-70.

uncomfortable, feeling ignorant and alone in the face of imminent spiritual peril. But just as suddenly the feeling goes away; the naïve young Protestant minister settles back in his chair, takes another sip of coffee, and thinks to himself how pleasurable it is to be in the company of truly educated people.

The two ministers' stories end up roughly similar, but with different implications. Like Robert Elsmere, Theron's slide from faith imperils his marriage and his living; he ends up deranged and destitute in New York City, on the brink of suicide. Unlike Elsmere, however, he does not salve his doubts by helping the poor and then succumbing to a noble death – in this thoroughly American tale, Theron Ware finds partial redemption selling real estate in the Pacific Northwest. Perhaps this is because Theron's realization has destroyed his hope of salvation. Abraham the Chaldean was not just different from the average Methodist minister – he was much, much worse.

History and Truth

The backstory to Theron Ware's problem is worth lingering over for a moment. Over the long run, the historicizing of biblical people and stories would have enormous implications for people of faith. There was no walking back from the realization that the men and women of the Bible lived in worlds governed by a different logic, entirely separate from the present. For some this meant that that the Bible was merely historical, with relatively little universal moral truth for people in other times and places. If Abraham was a Semitic nomad or the judges of Israel merely local warlords, then why in the world put their stories into a modern Sunday school curriculum? Others insisted that enough archaeological research and study would show that the Scriptures were in fact historically correct. What seemed like inaccuracies in the biblical text would be eventually cleared by godly scholars — no need for the orthodox to worry. For others it meant that Christianity itself was up for grabs. How could the Bible be true if it was basically an ancient text, written by people trapped in their own chronological bubble? Even worse, if Jesus was a first-century Jewish peasant, limited by the biases of his time and place, then how was he also the savior of all humanity? Although these three conclusions seem worlds apart, they are similar in one fundamental way: in every case the trustworthiness of the Bible rests on its correspondence to the actual "facts" of non-biblical history.

The heart of the problem is the word "historical," and the way its meaning was changing during Theron Ware's time. Beginning with the sixteenth-century Reformation and up through the late nineteenth century, most Protestants had generally understood the Bible as a historical book, in the sense that they knew its stories took place in the past. But they did not see those lives as fundamentally different from their own. The "real world" and the biblical world were "inseparable," as historian Peter Thuesen explains; both were part of God's "all-encompassing providential universe." This does not mean, says Thuesen, that people believed they were literally inhabitants of the biblical Israel or the biological children of Abraham. They simply understood in a broad sense that their history and ancient Israel's history were continuous, "parts of the same truth," overlapping spiritually if not chronologically.[6] Believers were to "live ancient lives," in Puritan preacher John Cotton's wonderful phrase, find-

6. Peter Thuesen, *In Discordance with the Scriptures: American Protestant Battles Over Translating the Bible* (New York: Oxford University Press, 1999), pp. 6, 7. Thuesen draws from Hans Frei, *The Eclipse of Biblical Narrative: A Study in Eighteenth and Nineteenth Century Hermeneutics* (New Haven: Yale University Press, 1974).

ing their bearings for the future by grounding themselves in the sacred biblical past.[7]

This is a challenging idea and perhaps a bit hard to grasp. Most of us see people from the Bible like Abraham or the apostle Paul as characters in stories, and we have learned to take into account the differences between their time and ours. We can receive inspiration or understanding from reading about them in the Bible, but we know their lives were separate. The older understanding of biblical people as somehow part of our lives reflects an older and less chronological sense of time, and the possibility that "then" and "now" could overlap and intersect in surprising ways.

Historicist thinking changed all this. Beginning in the eighteenth century, scholars began to look at the Bible as they would any other historical book. They began to delve more deeply into the stories of the ancient Israelites and the gospel accounts of Jesus, looking for physical evidence of supernatural events like the ten plagues or the miracle of the loaves and fishes. They came armed with knowledge of ancient languages – Aramaic, Hebrew, and Chaldean – and picks and shovels for archaeological exploration. Their work required rigorous sifting of ancient biblical texts for inaccuracies or inconsistencies, because these scholars aimed to put the old sacred stories into a modern chronological framework. They used their best research tools to pinpoint the probable year (within the western calendar of B.C. and A.D.) of historical events, like Abraham's departure from Ur of the Chaldees, or when the Israelites reached the Promised Land. When this evidence did not materialize – when scholars did not come up with independent factual proof in the annals of Egyptian history and archaeology for ten plagues, for example – then believers were faced with a prob-

---

7. Theodore Dwight Bozeman, *To Live Ancient Lives: The Primitivist Dimension in Puritanism* (Williamsburg: Institute of Early American History and Culture / Chapel Hill: University of North Carolina Press, 1988), p. 14.

lem. It looked like the Bible was not "true," in the sense that its accounts did not correspond directly to a separate historical "reality." It did not fit into the new logic of secular time.

By historical reality, of course, we mean the particular view of the past established by scholars. Using the texts and physical objects that people had left behind, and placing them within a logical framework of cause and effect, historians could claim that their view of the past was more "true" — more reliable according to the evidence at hand — than ancient attempts at explaining the unknown. And if the historical events in the Bible did not actually take place, at least as believers had learned to imagine them, then who was to say where the inaccuracies stopped? If Moses did not write the first five books of the Bible, as was long believed, then can we assume that the apostle Paul wrote the books ascribed to him in the New Testament? Or that Jesus actually said the words of the Gospels?[8]

The problem did not end there. The issue was not just whether biblical accounts were true, but whether they had any supernatural meaning. Historical thinking carried with it the assumption that every part of the past was a human product, created by people with their own unique view of the world. Taken to its logical conclusion, historicism also meant that the Bible and the Christian faith were not special: nothing stood outside the rules of historical context, not even a sacred book fundamental to the Christian faith. Not just music and art and politics were culturally determined; so was Christianity itself. The Eucharist was a rite copied from a bloody first-century mystery cult and the resurrection of Jesus an idea borrowed from the Egyptian legend of Osiris, a divine figure who came back to life after suffering pain and betrayal. By that reasoning, even the gospel hymns and altar calls in evangeli-

8. Thuesen, *In Discordance with the Scriptures*, pp. 6-10f.

cal churches were no less exotic than a ziggurat from ancient Persia or a psalm to Zeus.

The implications ran even further than that. Perhaps, as radical thinkers like Karl Marx, Sigmund Freud, and Auguste Comte suggested, God himself was one of those human products. Perhaps God was merely an authority figure wielded by the powerful against the rights of the working class, or a gigantic projection of our needs and desires — a fellow-member, in other words, of the modern bounded universe.

It is not always easy to track these kinds of changes, especially in the lives of individual people. But we do have some evidence that by the turn of the century historians were becoming particularly harsh religious skeptics. In 1916 a researcher, James Leuba, published a stunning survey of the religious beliefs of American intellectuals, from physical and biological scientists to social scientists, historians, and philosophers. Leuba grouped these scholars into two categories, "greater" and "lesser" men, separating those who taught at leading research universities from the plodders eking out a living in small, obscure colleges. All told, belief in God and immortality was not the majority view among any of the highly educated, but among "greater" historians, it was held by less than one-third. This was the same proportion as among the "greater" scientists, a hard-headed group expected to contain a high proportion of unbelievers. Though some historians, particularly the "lesser" ones, "continued to see the hand of God in human affairs," Leuba assumed that this number would decline with the rise of more rigorous standards of research and analysis.[9]

The ultimate casualty of historicism, then, was God. Historians did not need any divine help to explain why wars and famines

9. James Leuba, *The Belief in God and Immortality* (Boston: Sherman French and Co., 1916), pp. 261, 280.

took place: they were caused by economic shortages or population shifts, failed diplomatic alliances or new technology. This was not just a theoretical idea; for many people living through these changes a hundred or more years ago, it required an enormous shift in thinking. Historicism changed everything from Sunday school curricula to the ways churches celebrated anniversary years; it cropped up in Sunday sermons and denominational newspapers. It became *the* way to think about the world.

Returning for a moment to Theron Ware and his dilemma, we can begin to see how historical thinking changed the way all of modern western culture, including people of faith, look back at the past. Like Ware reading about Abraham, we assume that we are better and more enlightened than people who have lived before us. We are much higher on the ladder of time, looking out on a much larger landscape than they would have believed possible down on those murky bottom rungs. Thus, for example, while everyone who has lived before, including Chaldeans as well as Founding Fathers, allowed slavery and the oppression of women, we have grown beyond such unenlightened attitudes. Attitudes in the past were simply "primitive."

This kind of unquestioned faith in progress, central to the eighteenth-century Enlightenment's rebellion against religion, was all but universal a hundred or more years ago. Back then Americans, and many Europeans, simply assumed that the world was on a path of endless improvement. Why would they think otherwise? Until the great catastrophes of the twentieth century, holocausts and world wars, famines and plagues, the idea made a rough kind of sense. All of the technological and intellectual advances of the era — telephones and railroads and electricity and indoor plumbing — meant that people were getting smarter and life was getting better. The story of the United States itself made the case perfectly: here was an empty wilderness transformed by pioneers and inventors and business tycoons into the most advanced society on earth.

Though we are much more chastened in our confidence today, having gone through a century of wars and holocausts, we still hold to the basic assumption that today is always superior to yesterday. We assume that our ancestors don't have all that much to teach us; after all, they were "old-fashioned" and bigoted and they rarely washed or changed their clothes. They could not possibly be as thoughtful or self-aware as we are today. In fact, putting our ancestors into modern situations is a good way to create a laugh: can you imagine Benjamin Franklin merging onto a four-lane highway or following the scoring in a professional basketball game? Or Shakespeare confronted with an in-box of emails and a string of calls on his answering machine?

I daresay that for many people this is the main reason history seems irrelevant. All those stories about the Crusades or Roman gladiators seem pointless except as a way of reminding us about the horrible cruelties once believed acceptable behavior. The problem is even worse when we consider that the people of the Bible practiced all kinds of things that right-thinking people now frown upon — war and polygamy and even circumcising baby boys.

The Strange Becomes Familiar

Several years ago, well before sunrise on Easter Sunday, I was standing in a crowd of strangers, waiting for a glimpse of Jesus. People were huddling and stamping their feet against the cold of early spring, fingering rosaries and quieting fretful babies. They were also chain smoking, kissing, laughing, and flirting. In fact a good number of them looked like they were nursing terrible hangovers — but instead of wending their way back to bed they were, like me, waiting for Jesus.

This was Holy Week in Seville, Spain, an endlessly confusing, often puzzling, but always awe-inspiring way into Easter Sunday. All week, religious processions the like of which I had never seen, much less imagined, crisscrossed the city. Each one featured two enormous floats or *pasos*, carried by groups of men from Seville's many Catholic parishes, a day-long round trip from the church to the city cathedral and then back again. The journey began when the *paso* emerged from the church in an enormous cloud of incense to the squealing of an enthusiastic brass band. Every procession featured one ornate scene — some might say overwrought — from Christ's passion, complete with eye-rolling centurions and weeping women, and Christ himself fully prepared to die for the sins of humanity. Immediately after, the Virgin followed in her own *paso* wearing a richly brocaded white gown, surrounded by candles and flowers and covered by a beautifully embroidered canopy. Each procession was accompanied by "penitents" marching silently alongside. They all wore long robes and tall pointed hats, their faces covered except for two small slits for their eyes. Some of them carried tall white candles or wooden crosses and others waved canisters of incense as they passed by. Looking (to an American) for all the world like a phalanx of the Ku Klux Klan, the marchers carried bags of candy and holy cards to toss to the children in the crowds lining the streets.

At first all I could think of were my Dutch Calvinist ancestors, who would have recoiled from these scenes in horror. I felt very tall and pale and awkward in crowds of Spaniards, never quite sure what to do with my hands or where to look. I had been brought up to believe that Roman Catholics were not quite Christians in the way that we were; while we really *believed* the gospel, they just attended Mass — or even worse, it was whispered, they worshiped idols.

But no one acted that way during Holy Week in Seville. I saw a young mother introducing her one-year-old to the Virgin high up on her ornate *paso*, and I saw the little boy offer a shy smile and a wave, as if he were meeting a special aunt or grandmother. I saw the group of loud, fidgeting teenagers, who had been annoying me no end as we waited for a procession to leave the church, suddenly stand still and cross themselves when the church doors opened with great billows of incense and flickering candles. For that entire week in Seville I did not witness one ironic smirk or irreverent giggle, even from the most hung-over partygoers.

So much of the experience didn't make sense to me. Certainly the tormented man at the center of all those processions could not possibly be Jesus — not the Jesus I presumed I knew, anyway.

Over time I began to figure this out. I realized that Holy Week in Spain resonated with another emotionally powerful event in my life: sitting in a hospital waiting room after the sudden death of a dear friend. Everything about that time was surreal, of course, with people coming and going, some of them familiar — her family members and some of our mutual friends — and others who were complete strangers. These were the ones who confused me. Didn't they know that I was the number one friend, the one who knew Ginny the best? But here they were, unaware of me and just as stricken by shock and loss.

All those people knew different sides of my adventurous friend. They had climbed rock walls or hiked the Rocky Mountains with her, sat in her writing classes, or taught with her at different times in her life. My friend was Ginny the writer and hiker, the scholar with the ironic sense of humor. I had written books and organized conferences with her, chatted for hours over cups of coffee and plates of Indian food. Their friend was someone else entirely, the Ginny who spent the summer in a chalet high up in the Alps reading French novels or Ginny the neighborhood mom.

And unless I was prepared to share my friend with other people, I would never really know her.

The same was true of Jesus in Seville. Like my friends in the hospital waiting room, the people lining the streets to see those *pasos* go by knew the same Jesus I did but from another corner of Christian experience. Neither of us was wrong or right – who could ever claim to have the final word on the son of God? – and unless I could find a way to share him in Seville I would miss an incredible opportunity to know him in a deeper and more authentic way.

That experience of the familiar suddenly becoming strange, both in Seville and in that hospital waiting room, is why we need to know the stories of the past. "Good historical writing," says Archbishop Rowan Williams, engages us with the "strangeness of the past," all those differences, both huge and subtle, that make us both uncomfortable and in the end more self-aware.[10] Instead of dismissing the past as foreign or ridiculing it as odd and strange, we have the opportunity to embrace and perhaps even enjoy its oddities. Instead of plunging into worry when our ancestors do not emerge as carbon-copy versions of ourselves, we can give them the freedom to be different. In the end they will tell us far more about ourselves than we ever thought possible.

History for Grown-Ups

My husband used to ask me for historical examples to illustrate points in his Sunday sermons, but he doesn't do that anymore. Every time I came up with a decent story about loving your enemies

10. Rowan Williams, *Why Study History? The Quest for the Historical Church* (Grand Rapids: Eerdmans, 2005), pp. 23-24.

or practicing forgiveness, I immediately thought of a thousand qualifications. Yes, you could say that the Christians who fought against slavery were agents of God's grace — but their heads were also full of attitudes about race that would never pass muster today. They may have been champions of abolition, but most of them drew the line firmly at interracial marriage. And sure, John Winthrop and the Massachusetts Bay Puritans were wonderfully godly people who established a famous "city on a hill," but they also kept slaves and went to war against Native Americans with equally passionate zeal. Not surprisingly, few of my examples ever found their way into a sermon.

This does not mean that the past has no spiritual significance. Discovering that great saints failed to avoid the pitfalls of their time may make us cynical, but it can also make us wiser about our common human condition. All told, they are no worse and no better than us. Our ancestors may have fought brutal wars, but we invented — and have used — weapons capable of killing hundreds of thousands of people in an instant. They may have lived in closer harmony with nature than we do, but handicapped-access ramps and humane treatment for mental illness are inventions of our own age.

Historical perspective should make us more humble and cautious about ourselves. People from the past were not the only ones operating with a cultural context — we have one, too. Just like them we cannot imagine life any other way than it is: everyone assumes that "what is" is what was meant to be. And don't forget: the other side to this is the certainty that our own descendents will be shaking their heads in disbelief about all the impossible things we took for granted and the evils we accepted without protest — professional football perhaps, or maybe even amusement parks.

This does not mean giving our ancestors a free pass, however. It would be unfair to judge them by standards they would have no way of anticipating – it is too much, I think, to expect Puritans to be feminists or medieval bishops to be champions of religious tolerance. These ideas have come about today, in very incomplete and partial form, as the result of long and complex battles – through the processes of history itself. But at the same time, simply throwing up our hands and assuming that we have no right to criticize is more than a little patronizing. Twenty-first-century people are not the only ones to have grasped the problems of their time, or who have wished for a better world. In fact, that wish for justice and peace is probably more of a connecting thread across time than most of us realize.

History for grown-ups is complicated. It asks us to balance sympathy and judgment, hero-worship and sharp-eyed criticism. It recognizes and respects differences across time, but also looks for honest points of connection. Approached this way, the study of history is every bit as challenging as a trip to another country. As the world becomes a bigger and more complex place, and as we begin to locate ourselves on a bigger and more complex map of time, we become more understanding and empathetic people.

Our ancestors have a lot to teach us. This is not because they were wiser or more devout than we are or were "better" Christians, though we can't rule out such possibilities. It is because they can point us toward what is essential. Believers in every age have "majored in the minors," insisting that some truth or some practice was make-or-break for everyone. Over the course of two thousand years Christians have scoured the Bible for answers on everything from the proper use of icons to bicycles on Sunday, from the divinity of Christ to whether women should wear hats to church. In the course of my own research I have read more biblical arguments about the role of women than any person probably should, a span of records covering the past two centuries. At this point I can only sigh at the endless repetition of the same points over and over again — no one was reading any of the minutes from the previous meeting, apparently — and wonder when Christian people will recognize how this debate has distracted them from far more challenging matters, including the demands of love and justice. Here is a case where their blindness as well our own point us toward what is essential in our mutual Christian faith. Underneath all those battles, which seemed to mean so much at the time, is the essential meaning of the gospel.

In the end, history is not about sorting the good people from the bad, or the real believers from the frauds, as if we had a God's-eye view across time and space. It is not about finding allies to support our personal judgments or the particular causes of our time. Historical perspective is a way of knowing ourselves, of seeing more clearly the strengths and weaknesses of our Christian faith as it has been shaped by the demands of the early twenty-first century.

Things That Go Bump in the Night

It also invites us to see our ancestors within a framework of expectation.

For a long time, I freely admit, my favorite cable television vice has been ghost-chasers. These are reality-TV programs about investigators in search of hard evidence for the paranormal. Ghost hunters come in many different varieties. Some are intent on "debunking" so-called hauntings, pointing out rational reasons for a shadow on the ceiling or why the front door slammed in the middle of the night. Others are true believers, hearing messages from the great beyond in the smallest rustle of noise or shadowy flicker. But all of them make use of the latest in electronic technology, setting up motion-detectors and digital tape recorders in dark hallways and creepy attics, hoping to catch some sign of life on the other side.

Most of the time, the ghost hunters come up empty. In fact, despite the scary premise, the episodes actually tend to be fairly dull after a while, a half-hour of stomping around in the dark and then another half-hour of scanning video and sound recordings for a fleeting mist or a tiny background whisper. And if by chance the electronic equipment happens to catch a voice from the other side, they aren't terribly communicative – most of the time the ghostly message seemed to be on the order of "get out of here" or "leave me alone."

But I keep watching, mostly because of the possibility that something might actually happen. Maybe Great Aunt Mabel will materialize in the upstairs bedroom and ask everyone to tea, or a murder victim will name her killer while all the static night-vision cameras run. Because of that, I settle for the occasional jiggling door handle, because there's always the hope of something amazing out there in the hallway.

This is how I have come to understand history and faith. Instead of rock-bottom certainties about God's providence, I am more than happy to accept a bit of mystery. Instead of making hard and fast judgments about the righteousness or sin of the past, I prefer to live with surprises. History is not the reason I am a Christian – I do not look for evidence of God's will in events or expect people to act as personal role models. History is not about tidy moral lessons that will make us wiser and better in the present. If I thought about history this way, I will always end up confused or disappointed. Instead I hope for grace, that somewhere in the complicated mess of human events, someone will stand up, look around, and figure out how to do the right thing. I hope for someone to have the wits or courage to look up and wonder what is really going on. And I hope that in some way I will find a way to do that myself.

Letting the past speak for itself, as something much more than our private corral of truth or an occasion for cynicism, is a central part of what we might call *righteous remembering*. It means granting our ancestors the same critical judgment and forgiveness we want from others in our own lives. It means allowing mystery as an element of hope.

CHAPTER THREE

Memory Loss

On a frigid January evening in 1862, the Winslow Street Church in Taunton, Massachusetts, celebrated its twenty-fifth anniversary. That was not a startling event, especially in New England, where many churches measured time in centuries rather than decades; but it was a great occasion in Taunton, a small factory town near the Rhode Island border. The local paper reported that the town hall meeting room was "transformed into a mammoth tea-table" and its pillars draped with evergreens. Four hundred people gathered in that small room, enjoying a potent mixture of laughter, music, poetry, and pious memories. They sampled from the tables groaning with roast turkey, potatoes, homemade bread, apple pies, and hot drinks for those coming in from the chill. They gasped with delight to see old friends and family back in Taunton after years away.

At the center of the room, in the spot normally reserved for the town ballot box, was a pulpit, and on it a large Bible. The pulpit came from Winslow Street's original building and had been brought out to mark the anniversary celebration. The Bible was a gift from John Reed, a deeply beloved founder of the church, long since dead.

After the food had been piled onto plates and the hugs and greetings mostly taken care of, the room quieted down and the guests drew up their chairs into a circle. And then the older members began to reminisce. One by one the old folks told their stories, some humorous and some sad, but most of them about John Reed. One elderly gentleman had very clear memories of the congregation's humble beginning in "John Reed's School Room," where the old saint had taught Bible stories and urged his students to turn their lives over to God. Others joined him in equally emotional reminiscences about "our Mount of Beatitudes" in that small sacred space. This was where many of them had first encountered God for the first time as children, and the lingering sense of awe brought a hush to the crowded room.

Then with a great rustle of skirts, a tall woman – one of John Reed's family members, in fact – came forward to read a poem. With a mock solemn flourish she pulled a long sheet of paper from her dress pocket and announced the title of her composition, "Past-Present." "There's no dead Past," Mrs. Reed began, "except for those who in life's web were only shoddy," spending too much time "with capon, turtle soup, and toddy." Her tone grew a bit more earnest as she continued. Only those with eyes to see, she said, could recognize "the savor/Of good deeds done, of good words spoken,/ Their line by centuries unbroken." Then came the final stanzas: because those "good words and deeds can never die," even biblical figures like Paul and Peter were "now more alive than ever." In fact, she said, Moses himself lives on. Although "his grave/Remains unfound in Moab's valley," he is still "ready to lead the final rally."[1]

Amid appreciative nods and applause, the author returned to her seat. Probably no one minded the awkward rhythms or even the length of Mrs. Reed's poem, which I have quoted *very* selectively. But the other reason why the audience listened so intently to the poem was because Mrs. Reed was, for most of them, family.

During this time in American history, members of small-

---

1. *The First Quarter Century of the Winslow Church: Containing a Historical Discourse, Preached January 12, 1862* (Taunton, Mass., 1862), pp. 50-51, 53, 55, 57-61, 66-67.

town churches were often relatives, sometimes many times over, bound together in a complex network of marriages and births. Church was the center of social life, where young men and women stole glances at future spouses during the hymn and later brought their children for baptism. On the Sunday morning following the gala, when the minister launched into a carefully researched sermon telling the history of the church, he was talking about people whose actual descendants were sitting together in rows of wooden pews right in front of him.

That evening in Taunton, the family circle widened even further to include John Reed himself. As people talked about him he became real to them, in his own way still a member of the Winslow Street Church. John Reed was not just "back there" in some strange land of the past, but still in relationship with the present-day congregation. Memories of John Reed made people feel closer together, more united to meet the challenges ahead. In other words, this man, though long dead, was still alive to those living in Taunton, Massachusetts, in 1862.

"We live in the past as well as in the future," a Geneva, New York, Presbyterian pastor told his congregation in 1859. This is an attitude we don't generally encourage today, but to this minister and his people it was essential to a life of faith. The Geneva church was a small rural outpost with about 400 members, nothing terribly out of the ordinary as far as nineteenth-century Presbyterians were concerned. But if we consider "all the souls of this great congregation for two generations" – he reckoned this number around 1,850 people – and all of the sermons and prayers of the ministers who had filled the pulpit, the Presbyterian Church of Geneva was downright formidable.[2]

---

2. Hubbard Winslow, *The Former Days: History of the Presbyterian Church of Geneva* (Boston: Crocker and Brewster, 1859), pp. 14, 27-28.

Those former church members set a high standard for the living. In fact, some ministers enjoyed having their congregations imagine their grandparents slogging through all kinds of weather to attend the Sunday service. As one Connecticut pastor intoned, "the soaking rain and the driving storm of snow were matters of little account with the hardy ancestors of this settlement." Unlike their sluggish descendants, these godly men and women believed that going to church was an "indispensable duty." "Alas!" he cried, "that the good habit should ever have been laid aside."[3] Some ministers went even further in making their parishioners squirm. At the two-hundredth anniversary of a church in Quincy, Massachusetts, the minister had his congregation imagine all of their former pastors rising up from "yonder burying ground," and marching "in ghostly procession up this aisle to this altar." We can imagine a certain amount of uncomfortable shifting in the pews as the pastor put the question to them: "what think ye would be the lessons that would be uttered by those ministers of Christ?"[4]

But the ancestors were not always disgruntled. Just as often they brought strength and encouragement. "What connection, if any, departed spirits have with this world, we know not," Braintree pastor Richard Storrs told a group of mourners at a funeral service in 1847. We cannot know for sure "whether they are ministering spirits to their surviving friends, or are employed on errands of love to other parts of the universe." But Storrs did not doubt in the least that the dead were being kept busy "furthering the great de-

3. *History of the First Ecclesiastical Society in East Windsor, From its Formation in 1852, to the Death of its Second Pastor, Rev. Shubael Bartlett in 1854* (Hartford: Case, Tiffany and Co., 1857), pp. 21, 22.

4. *Two Discourses, Delivered September 29, 1839, on Occasion of the Two Hundredth Anniversary of the Gathering of the First Congregational Church, Quincy, Massachusetts, . . . by William P. Lunt* (Boston: James Munroe and Co., 1840), p. 57.

signs of God, and carrying out into execution his vast purposes of benevolence." Somehow, for these industrious New Englanders the idea of godly people lying around with nothing to do, even though they were dead, was just not acceptable. "It seems to me," a seminary professor told a funeral gathering in 1848, "that the saints in heaven will be as much more active than they ever were in this world, as they are more holy, and more benevolent, and endued with higher powers. They will be full of action, because they will be full of love."[5]

Obviously the Taunton reunion is a long way from church celebrations in the present. Most of us do not enjoy flowery speeches any more than we salivate at the prospect of "capon, turtle soup, and toddy." Nor do we launch over-the-top sentimental tributes to our Sunday school teachers or roll out their Bibles for public viewing. And when we tally up the membership numbers of our churches, we never include those dead or gone. Once people die they are automatically dropped from the list.

What is most striking about the churches in Taunton and Geneva is the confidence that history was *real*. The past and its people still figured in their daily lives, and especially in their life of faith. In fact, in a way, "invisible friends" like John Reed remind us of medieval Catholic saints. Of course no nineteenth-century Protestant would have ever prayed to Mr. Reed or expected a miraculous answer; they would not go on pilgrimages to visit his relics (though there were some echoes of this at Winslow Street). But

5. Richard Storrs, *A Discourse Delivered at Stoughton, Mass., at the Funeral of Rev. Calvin Park, D.D. on Friday January 8, 1857* (Andover: Allen, Morrill and Wardwell, 1847), p. 10; Augustus C. Thompson, *Better Land; or, the Believer's Journey and Future Home* (Boston: Gould and Lincoln, 1859), p. 205; Leonard Woods, *The Heaven of Christians: A Sermon Delivered at the Funeral of Mrs. Phebe Farrar, wife of Samuel Farrar, Esq., Andover, Mass., January 26, 1848* (Andover: William H. Wardwell, 1848), pp. 16-17.

both believed that the ancestors were still relevant to the lives of people in those communities.[6]

This is part of the world we have lost. Today many of us have only a hazy sense of our family history back more than two generations, and we live in towns and cities that exist only in the present. The old saints in our churches are just names on a stained glass window or meeting hall, honoring them for a donation of money or a bequest. We run across them on marble plaques listing those who died in World War I or World War II, or as honorees in Easter lily or poinsettia displays during holidays. But all in all they are strangers, even though they once sat in the very pews and looked out the same windows as we do on Sunday mornings.

Why do these people mean so little? Why do we no longer remember them in the ways that the people of Taunton and Geneva did, just barely a century and a half ago? In this chapter we take up the problem of remembering itself. For many of us our memories become an issue when we are trying to connect a name with a face at a dinner party or searching for our car keys. But there is much more to it than that. Today the various mechanisms for remembering are being explored in neuroscience laboratories and psychological tests, as well as in gatherings of social scientists, philosophers, and historians. Though their questions and answers are different, they agree on one point: memory is not an automatic process, involving only certain routine functions of the brain. Our sense of the past is profoundly shaped by our individual experiences and by the worlds we inhabit. Whether we are members of a tribe without a written history or avid users of the latest communication technology, our memories are — at least in part — the product of our surroundings.

6. "Invisible friends" comes from Peter Brown, *The Cult of the Saints: Its Rise and Function in Latin Christianity* (Chicago: University of Chicago Press, 1981), p. 63.

We can even say that memory has a history. It takes on different forms as the world grows more modern; as social situations change, the "how," "why," and "what" of remembering change as well. This is another fairly abstract idea, however, and best illustrated with another story, this one taking place decades after those two celebrations, just before the opening of the twentieth century.

Imagining the Past

This episode begins on an ocean pier on a bright summer day in 1896, as twenty-four American tourists set out for England, the land of the Pilgrim Fathers. Despite the historical theme, their trip bore little resemblance to the perilous voyage of 1620. The "reverse pilgrimage" of 1896 was the height of luxury, passed in the comfort of an ocean liner and the soft beds of plush hotels. Instead of prison cells and burning stakes, these pilgrims encountered nothing but the best in English hospitality, greeted everywhere by lord mayors, bishops, and society figures.

The modern pilgrims also found plenty of opportunity for fun. "They pretend that they are pilgrims of the stock and times of Scrooby and Plymouth Rock," one American newspaper told its readers. For some reason this meant presenting their English hosts with a wooden crusaders' staff tied with apple-blossoms, ribbons, and a lady's fan. Everyone appeared to be in on the joke: according to the newspaper account the gesture was "accepted with solemn gravity" and an "irrepressible twinkle."[7] The reverse pilgrims also had no intentions of overdosing on piety. After a few weeks in England, the group crossed over to Holland for a whirlwind tour

---

7. Advertisements, *The Congregationalist*, 7 January 1897; review in *The Interior*, 24 December 1896.

of Rotterdam, Leiden, and Amsterdam, and then on to the spas of Germany and the grand avenues of fin de siècle Paris.

In fact the travelers had all kinds of fun outside the usual itinerary of a religious pilgrimage. This much is clear in a letter written by Morton Dexter, one of the party who stayed in England while the rest of the group went on to the Continent. "I am as lonely . . . as an anti-tobacco lecturer in Germany," he complained to them. And though, Dexter mock-chided, I have tried to exert an "ennobling influence" on you all, reports from your trip across the English Channel suggest that my lessons were in vain. According to what I hear, "only a few hours after you left me, you all . . . were 'half seas over,'" downing large doses of "Dutch courage." "And this, too," moaned Dexter, "so soon after partaking of the cheering, but not inebriating hospitalities of Lady Henry Somerset." (Lady Henry Somerset was a leader of Britain's prohibition movement.) "I beseech you to pause ere it becomes too late," he declared. "Beware the flowing bowl – especially aboard ship!"[8]

Apparently they knew how to have a good time. The twenty-four included a sprinkling of clergymen and wealthy lay people; nine of the men were single professionals – doctors and lawyers mostly – and most of the twelve single women were society dames from Hartford, Connecticut. The religious newspaper sponsoring the trip reported that the participants had been chosen for their "marked Puritan and Pilgrim sympathies," but above all as people "who would be congenial" and would value "the unusual privileges to be offered them."[9]

In one sense their trip was all about history. The tour included all the famous spots of East Anglia, the original home of the New England Puritans. Before they fled to the Continent the visitors at-

8. Morton Dexter to the Party, 4 July 1896, Congregational Library Small Collections.

9. "The 'Congregationalist's' Pilgrims," *Congregationalist*, 4 June 1896, p. 900.

tended services in historic churches, posed in front of monuments and plaques, and listened to endless speeches about the significance of the Puritan heritage.

But in other ways, the trip had very little to do with the actual past. The visit to England did not retrace historic events or try to relive the perils and hardships of 1620; if anything the Pilgrims were incidental to the tour. The latter-day pilgrims were not looking for spiritual inspiration from their ancestors, and as the surviving evidence suggests, they did not find it, either. History did not spur pious reflection.

The past was a place to visit through the imagination. Rather than real people with their own separate lives, the ancestors were part of a make-believe land, characters in a play who could be made to talk and act in all kinds of different ways. In other words, historical accuracy was not the point in dealing with the past. There was no need for one-to-one correspondence between an event and the way it appeared in the present. Remembering was becoming something much more than a true recollection of real events. Cut loose from the rules of chronology and context, history was becoming fun.

As the twentieth century rolled on, historical celebrations became much more ornate and much more entertaining. Tolerance for long speeches and sermons began to fade, as audiences demanded something to look at, not just to hear. One favorite was the "tableau vivante," where costumed actors arranged themselves into a scene from a painting, usually depicting a famous historic event, and then held the pose in silence as long as they could. Though to us today this might have all the entertainment value of watching paint dry, given the alternative of a long didactic sermon, it was genuinely welcome.

Soon the tableau vivante was far too tame. In my wanderings through the stacks of the Congregational Library, I have found descriptions of all kinds of over-the-top celebrations honoring the

300th anniversary of the Pilgrims' arrival in Plymouth in 1620. In the late summer of 1920, the Massachusetts town of Truro remembered the Pilgrim Fathers with a gigantic stage show. The cast of characters included Indians, Mayflower voyagers, and several barefoot girls dressed in gauzy pastels, who swept across the stage at random intervals to convey the idea "that the Pilgrims felt the unseen." After the performance, the citizens of Truro dressed up as Pilgrims, carrying breech loading rifles and wearing buckled shoes and hats. With a photographer in tow they trudged earnestly across the hills of Cape Cod, pausing to strike poses for the benefit of posterity, and for their photographer. In one spot they pantomimed delight over discovering the stash of buried corn that kept the first settlers alive in 1620; in another they recoiled in dismay as the Indian chief "Samoset" took the heroic "John Winslow" hostage.[10]

From there the past became as spectacular as modern imaginations could conceive, celebrated with parades and floats, pageants and enormous theatrical productions. In Omaha, the state of Nebraska launched a full parade of floats with citizens depicting the "Persecution of the Pilgrim Fathers," the "Landing on Cape Cod" – and for good measure the Boston Tea Party and the Goddess of Liberty.[11] By the 1920s, audiences loved pageants that ended with an over-the-top flourish, such as the one that featured a group of Adventurous Spirits "dressed in the colors of the sunset and dancing to alluring music," and a procession of "goldseekers, pioneers, Puritan clergymen, woodmen, trappers, and Jesuits" following them westward across the stage.[12]

10. Frederick Brooks Noyes, "The Call of the Cape," *Congregationalist*, 16 September 1920, pp. 342-43.

11. "A Notable Pilgrim Parade in Omaha," *Congregationalist*, 9 December 1920, p. 738.

12. Esther Willard Bates, *A Pageant of Pilgrims* (Boston: Pilgrim Press, 1920), pp. v, vi.

In the years that followed Americans learned to enjoy the past in other imaginative ways. They flocked to see Hollywood costume epics, with movie stars playing Cleopatra or Joan of Arc, Mark Anthony or King Arthur. They cheered as Judah Ben Hur wheeled his chariot around a Roman coliseum and wept as he took a cup of water from none other than Jesus Christ himself. Even today, people who would never sit through a lesson on Scottish history thrill to see Mel Gibson rallying his men for battle, all dressed in authentic plaid and blue body paint. Millions of people have watched the *Titanic* sink in historically correct fashion, taking down real people like millionaires John Jacob Aster and Isidor Straus as well as fictional lovers Rose Bukater and Jack Dawson.

What happened in the years between the Winslow Street celebration and the reverse pilgrimage to Europe? The two stories, not historically significant in themselves, are examples of important changes taking place in western culture, ones that would forever transform the way we look at the past.

Puritans on Roller Coasters

We can explore this change by going back to the amusement park, a parable of modern culture we looked at in chapter one. The endlessly repeatable thrill of a Ferris wheel or a merry-go-round illustrated the discipline of time, as a never-changing progression from past to present to future. But we (or perhaps I) shouldn't overlook the fact that amusement parks were meant to be fun. From Coney Island and Disney World to the rickety rides at the county fair, they are places to forget your watch and calendar and happily meander from one experience of fun to the next.

We tend to take this experience for granted, as a perfectly acceptable form of innocent enjoyment — but we don't have to go too far back in time to find an entirely different set of attitudes. There is a good reason why you cannot imagine one of the Pilgrim Fathers kicking back at Six Flags, or Daniel Boone going down a water slide. It is not that their lives were busier than ours, or that they were more serious people. We are all busy in our own ways, whether we are hunting down dinner in a forest or laboring through the crowds at our local supermarket. The difference is in our attitudes toward leisure time.

Today reading a novel or going to see a play is just a way to pass the time, and a fairly admirable one at that, given the alternatives of video games and reality television. Two hundred years ago, however, a decent man or woman would not have wasted God-given time with people and events that had never taken place, and in a manner designed to artificially stimulate the emotions. The theatre is "wholly *useless*," a minister told his flock in 1825. "Can it teach the mechanic industry, or the merchant more economy and skill?" Surely not, he declared. Even at its very best, the theatre is "mere *recreation*."[13]

Now entire industries have grown up around our increasingly sophisticated needs for relaxation and entertainment: video games and movies, vacation homes and resorts, golf courses and professional sports. This is not because we are lazier than our ancestors across the board; lazy people can be found anywhere. What has changed is the way we have access to the fun itself, the assumption that amusement is something we can buy and own.

This is another central feature of the modern world we inhabit. Especially since the turn of the last century, we have become a society "preoccupied with consumption," as one historian has described it, "with comfort and bodily well-being, with luxury,

---

13. *On Theatrical Exhibitions: A Sermon, Delivered in Utica, December 11, 1825, by Rev. S. C. Aiken* (Utica: Colwell and Wilson, 1825), pp. 12, 13.

spending, and acquisition, with more goods this year than last, more next year than this."[14] All around us, advertisements and commercials urge us on to the next new thing; our conversations always seem to circle back to something we have bought or want to buy some day. We are all fairly familiar with the evils of our consumer culture — the crassness, excess, and reduction of everything into a commodity to be bought or sold — so I don't think it necessary to linger on this point (though we certainly could). The important thing here is to understand the way consumer culture has changed the way we connect to the past.

To begin with, a way of life based on the "new and improved" is by definition hostile to anything old. But more than that, the constant push toward the future undermines the power of traditions, whether they are an immigrant's Old World customs, small-town rituals like checker games at the old five-and-dime, or the sacred tenets of religious believers. Americans have always embraced the "next best thing" — this is the New World, after all — but consumer culture's view of the future is different. Rather than something to be imagined and built, that wonderful next best thing is something that can be bought and owned. Our problem is confusing "the good life with goods."[15]

Even the past itself is a commodity. Today people pay enormous amounts of money for old clocks and furniture, vintage clothing, and rare books — items that our grandparents and great-grandparents used every day without a second thought. Ironically, in this age of the new and improved, the flotsam and jetsam that surface at an antique auction becomes more valuable the older it gets. We also travel long distances to see old things. Millions of non-churchgoers line up to see the ancient cathedrals of England

14. William Leach, *Land of Desire: Merchants, Power, and the Rise of a New American Culture* (New York: Vintage Books, 1993), p. xiii.

15. Leach, *Land of Desire*, p. xiii.

and France, ready to be awed by sacred architecture – and then ushered through the gift shop on the way out. Here in Boston, history is no gentle pastime either – it is a business that the city depends on for its survival. The roughly 20 million tourists who walk the Freedom Trail every year and buy ice cream and sandwiches along the way generate an enormous amount, somewhere around $6 million, toward the tax revenues.

If the past is a consumer item, then so are its people. Or at the very least they are not three-dimensional men and women like we are. On Presidents' Day weekend George Washington and Abraham Lincoln are busy with car advertisements; on the Fourth of July the Founding Fathers urge Americans to take advantage of the shoe sale at the local mall. Other famous people from the past appear as bobblehead dolls, cartoon figures on billboards, and sometimes even giant balloons in parades.

These changes help us understand the difference between the celebration in Taunton and the reverse pilgrimage of 1896. For one, the ancestors were real and still present, and for the other they were imaginary characters. The "reverse pilgrims" did not feel a moral obligation to the Pilgrim Fathers, any more than the citizens of Taunton could have imagined play-acting their way across England and the Continent.

The History of Memory

The two stories demonstrate that remembering has a history, that its meaning and form have changed over time. Certainly in the centuries before the invention of the tape recorder – or paper, for that matter – people of every age and time have found different ways of connecting with the past, whether reliving the exploits of their ancestors around a campfire or gathering in front of a church pulpit for the minister's "historical discourse." Sometimes societies delegated certain people to be rememberers, relying on them to memorize long lists of genealogies and kingships, tasks too mentally challenging for ordinary people. The ancient Greeks appointed *mnemons* to keep track of important community matters like decisions in law courts and the religious calendar of feasts and sacrifices. In mythology and legend, the *mnemon* often accompanied a hero to remind him of the "divine mission that will cause his death if he forgets it."[16]

But generally speaking, the final responsibility for remembering fell to everyone as a whole. The very process of building collective memories created a sense of belonging to a tribe or a town or a faith, reminding them not only who they were but what made them different from all others. The narratives told by Maoris or Greeks or medieval Christians would have been as meaningless and foreign to outsiders as they would have been inspiring and precious to insiders.

Modern memory is different. We no longer expect that a particular set of memories is the sole property of a single group — those images of the past can belong to anyone. This is central to the idea of American citizenship, for example: new citizens learn the ins and outs of the Constitution but also the story of American history. Once all the papers and affidavits and oaths are taken care of, they have the same claim to George Washington and Abraham Lincoln as a lineal descendent of the Mayflower Pilgrims. As Americans they take on an entirely new "archive of memory," as one scholar has described it, not by being raised and trained with a national identity but by the simple act of swearing allegiance. It is now possible for an individual to "suture himself or herself into a

16. Jacques Le Goff, *History and Memory*, trans. Steven Rendall and Elizabeth Claman (New York: Columbia University Press, 1992), p. 63.

larger history," and in that way feel a connection to the past.[17] The process is hardly that simple in practice, but the principle behind it is very clear: American history is not the sole property of the native born, a story told to create an exclusive group identity, but a set of stories that are transferable. The struggles of the pioneers and the tragedy of Lincoln's assassination belong to newcomers by virtue of a loyalty oath to the United States. Once the story of the Pilgrims was the birthright of certain people in New England; today anyone can adopt that historic event, and the entire history of the United States, as their own, no matter how far they can trace their ancestry on American shores.

Today history belongs to everyone. It is not owned by a few highly educated professional scholars, people with the time and ability to conduct lengthy research projects. In many ways the past is remarkably and wonderfully accessible to the average person. Although most of us could not carry on much of a conversation with a nuclear physicist or molecular biologist, anyone can take a peek into the world of historians. Anyone can read about Harry Truman or Genghis Khan or join in debates about the Founding Fathers. White people can celebrate Black History Month in February and men can join in the festivities of Women's History Month in March. All of us can connect to the past through the power of the imagination. For some people this might mean reading a historical novel or watching a movie epic, and for others acquiring elaborate knowledge about Civil War uniforms and battles and then re-enacting a famous event. There are no strict rituals or rules to follow.

The imagined past is a great gift, but it also opens up a new set of problems. Events that can be celebrated with parade floats and

17. Alison Landsberg, *Prosthetic Memory: The Transformation of American Remembrance in the Age of Mass Culture* (New York: Columbia University Press, 2004), pp. 2, 3, 9.

movie stars in period costume are fun, but they can also become trivialized. They can reduce justly famous people into cartoons or stereotypes, someone to chuckle over rather than take seriously. This is not to say that we can never find the past funny or odd — it is, after all, populated by human beings — but I am pretty sure that years of watching Abraham Lincoln shill cars on Presidents' Day has made it difficult for the average high school student to understand the power of the Gettysburg Address or the tragedy of his assassination.

In a sense history is always about the imagination, since there is no way to travel to the past as we would to a foreign country. But there is a thin line between approaching people and events through imagination and assuming that they are in fact imaginary. The first assumes that the past was "real," with a separate integrity all its own; the second that there is no past at all beyond what we choose to see.

Are Memories Real?

What happens when a person remembers? Where do all those promises and driving directions and answers to test questions actually go? For centuries the answer was that memories existed somewhere in the mind — the Greeks used the image of a signet ring making an impression on hot wax — and lay there waiting until they were needed. In other words, our experiences from the past never go away, but for various reasons become inaccessible.

By the early twentieth century this view of memory had been bolstered by science. Scopolamine, for example, was a drug originally thought to help women with the pain of childbirth, but researchers soon discovered that it was far more effective in other settings. In the right dosages it would reduce inhibitions, and allow a person to let loose even the most carefully guarded secrets. "Truth serum" was not just a popular plot device in spy movies — it verified what most people assumed was true about memory, that somewhere in the recesses of the mind lay the "truth," just waiting to be unleashed. The most significant laboratory evidence came from the experiments of Wilder Penfield, a Canadian neuroscientist who worked with epileptic patients in the World War II era. He discovered that stimulating certain areas of the brain with electrodes would produce vivid recollections of past experiences, as if those were being stored away and under the right circumstances became fully accessible. Wilder's patients would actually see themselves at a childhood friend's birthday party or learning to drive a car, not as vague reminiscences, but so real that patients felt as if they were actually living through them again.[18] All this fueled the growing fascination with past lives and reincarnation, hugely popular in the nervous 1950s and adventurous 1960s. Like the Russian spy's secret code for the atom bomb, a waitress's former existence as a barbarian king or an Egyptian princess was all "in there," just waiting for the right prompting to come to the surface.

We are more skeptical now. Hard-nosed scientific experiments have shown that memories in fact change over time, taking on different shades of meaning as people pass through the ups and downs of life. What was once a happy reminiscence — meeting your future spouse for the first time, perhaps — might take on more sinister overtones after a messy divorce. Different family members may recall the practical details of a vacation trip in surprisingly different ways. Was the car blue or green? Did we actually spend the night in Yosemite?

18. Alison Winter, *Memory: Fragments of a Modern History* (Chicago: University of Chicago Press, 2012), pp. 82f.

Not only that, memories can also be made up on the spot, in response to the smallest amount of suggestion or pressure from a group. Psychologist Elizabeth Loftus has demonstrated the phenomenon of "group-think" over and over in her research. In one case, she presented her subjects with a random combination of photographs from recent news events, some of them subtly altered to show a different story. With very little guidance Loftus found, for example, that 31 percent of the people who saw a doctored photograph "remembered" that President George W. Bush was relaxing at his Texas ranch with baseball pitcher Roger Clemens during Hurricane Katrina. Almost 70 percent "remembered" very clearly that during the 2008 presidential campaign Hilary Clinton used Jeremiah Wright in a TV ad against Barack Obama. Even memories of our own lives seem infinitely pliable — after seeing themselves in a doctored photo, half of the college students in one study were convinced that they'd gone up in a hot air balloon as a child.[19]

By now we have all seen the implications of this view. In the 1990s a string of sex abuse charges against daycare workers, based on testimony from small children, landed many innocent people in prison. The stories were horrific, but hard to dismiss: after all, why would an innocent child remember anything but the truth? The trials and their aftermath brought us the phrase "false memory syndrome," the idea that those child witnesses could be made to remember events that never actually happened. All it took was the right kind of suggestion from an authority figure, even something as unintentional or small as a stray gesture or tilt of the head.

We are also used to seeing memory manipulated in political campaigns. The presidential election of 2004 gave us the verb "swiftboating," to describe the way Democratic candidate John

---

19. William Saletan, "The Ministry of Truth," http://slate.com/toolbar.aspx?action=print&id=2254054, accessed 9/16/10.

Kerry's Vietnam War record was shouted down and falsified by his opponents. Kerry's combat experience was a matter of public record, and he carried actual battle scars from enemy shells, but in an amazingly short span of time, millions of people believed that Kerry had either embellished or completely made up those established facts. The "big lie," as George Orwell called it, can be an enormously effective weapon.

Are there such things as authentic or "pristine" memories? Or are these all fleeting and subjective, constantly being made and remade as we respond to our surroundings and pile on layers of life experience? At this point, there is no hard and fast evidence that links memories to "true" accounts of the past. More and more, we are coming to understand memory as simply a process, an unstable combination of brain chemistry and social cues.[20]

E-Remembering

Daniel Bell thinks he has the answer. He is the author of a book called *Total Recall: How the E-Memory Revolution Will Change Everything*, and has decided that remembering is too important to leave to biology. In 1998 Bell developed an ingenious way of capturing his past without having to hold it in his head: he keeps a small digital camera around his neck — a SenseCam — to capture everything he encounters in the course of the day. His "lifelogging" also includes a digital recorder to capture every sound he hears and a scanner for everything he reads. Not surprisingly Bell also has a secretary who has helped him scan boxes and boxes of accumulated stuff, and then discards them after she is done. Everything from Bell's past, from T-shirt logos to engineering papers, has been off-

20. Winter, *Memory*, p. 257.

loaded into an inexpensive hard drive, a digital file that also includes records of hundreds of thousands of documents, emails, and phone calls. Our minds contain similar information, but only a tiny portion is available to us, even on a good day. Bell has a custom search engine that can retrieve his memories instantly. It can pinpoint a conversation from ten years ago or locate lost car keys; the smallest detail is quickly available. Bell has in a way overcome the problem of subjectivity.

The SenseCam is one end of a long arc in the history of memory. Before the invention of the printing press or the availability of cheap disposable paper, remembering was almost entirely an internal process: people had to store enormous amounts of information in their heads. By the late medieval period, memory experts had developed elaborate techniques for sorting and accessing all kinds of important facts, from biblical texts to lists of gambling debts. Memory became a game of skill and a highly valued art form. As books and paper became more widely available, memories became more and more external; important facts could be placed in a copy book or a library, captured on film, and broadcast to the world via television. Daniel Bell's memories are almost fully external, sitting in his hard drive. "It doesn't take much imagination," writes Jonathan Foer, who profiled Bell for a book on feats of memory, "to see how future versions of the SenseCam could be embedded in a pair of eyeglasses, or inconspicuously sewn into clothing, or even somehow tucked under the surface of the skin or embedded into a retina."[21]

We have come a long way from the Winslow Street Church. Remembering has become more democratic and open, free from our human tribalisms; but it is also becoming less valuable. If the

---

21. Jonathan Foer, *Moonwalking with Einstein: The Art and Science of Remembering Everything* (New York: Penguin Books, 2011), pp. 138-61.

only trustworthy memories are those in our personal archive, inaccessible and irrelevant to everyone else, then how is history, the story of a collective past, even possible? If memories are little more than fleeting fragments of biochemical processes, then how can we remember together?

CHAPTER FOUR

The Great Conversation

Just about everyone can remember a history teacher who nearly bored them to death. The class seemed to consist of little more than long lists of names and dates and presidents — information with no practical use other than for a future game show contestant. It is no accident that Harry Potter's history teacher at Hogwarts is literally a ghost, shuffling through the same piles of yellowed lecture notes year after year. Learning about the past can be painful.

Fear and loathing of history is everywhere. I have seen it in the tired and alienated faces of college freshmen taking a required introductory class and the nonplussed looks of perky people who ask me what I do for a living. I don't usually take offense: history *is* dull when it comes as a string of unrelated information, temporarily jammed into our memory banks in order to pass a test.

I suspect, however, that the fear and loathing draws on something much more significant than bad teaching. Any good teacher knows that there are plenty of ways to make history interesting to students: film clips and guest speakers and visits to museums, good texts and lively discussions. But all the teaching innovations in the world will not make it relevant to them. What does it matter to anyone sitting in a twenty-first-century classroom what some ancient medieval ruler said to his courtiers a thousand years ago?

By now we know that the reasons why we feel cut off from

or even bored by history are embedded into the "rules" of modern culture. We see time as a line that is constantly and inexorably moving forward, leaving our medieval king further and further in the rearview mirror. In fact, we even believe that time has a rhythm and a shape – we talk about it in terms of ripples of rise and decline, eras of swift change and slow-moving lulls, ages of great light and excitement and periods of lawless ignorance. Of course, all of this would be a novelty to the South American tribesman who points forward when he talks about the past. Neither of us knows what time "looks like," of course – our cultural assumptions about time are as much imagined as his, and just as deeply woven into the beliefs and practices we take for granted.

We also believe that from our end of this undulating timeline, we have a certain omnipotence. We can see the mistakes and blunders of the past far more clearly than the people who were living through them. In fact, we claim that studying history will help us learn from their mistakes and thus avoid repeating them. But even if we choose to ignore the "lessons of the past," we can still claim superiority over a benighted medieval king who thought the world was flat and that angels pushed the planets across the sky.

The only possible link across the divide of time separating this man from us is our imagination. We can visit the remains of his castle and sit on his throne, and perhaps for a moment this ancient figure will "come alive to us." He will become an image in the mind's eye, striding up and down his throne room with all the primitive pomp we would expect. But we do not need to visit him with a serious purpose in mind. We are not paying respects or necessarily all that curious about the particulars of his life. He is not a real person in the sense that we feel a moral obligation to him as we would to a living human being. He is not even a role model, good or bad: after all, he has been dead for hundreds of years.

And so, it seems, are all the assumptions about life that he once took for granted, the traditions that reflected his beliefs about the world. In the twenty-first century we do not feel any need to revere kings or pursue the rituals of courtly love. Fathers do not marry off their daughters to form alliances with other families, or enslave serfs to mow the lawn on Saturdays. And above all, we do not bend the knee to his God, a vengeful being who spoke through bishops and popes and demanded crusades against pagans and Saracens.

In a larger sense, this disconnect is true about all of the "old ways" in the modern world: they carry no weight of obligation on us the living. If we choose, we can embrace old practices which might enrich everyday life or perhaps provide a sense of connection to something larger than ourselves – but nothing says we have to. We might put on a full-out Christmas celebration from the Old Country (wherever it might be), with special food and clothes and customs drawn from increasingly hazy family memories. At the same time we are perfectly free to skip the extras and enjoy a "regular" Christmas like everyone else.

Tradition is a choice. Some people enjoy sampling the old ways through folk dancing or obscure kinds of cooking, or rough it for a week or two in a country cabin without electricity or running water. A few of the more forward-looking tourist agencies are even offering travel packages for people who want to experience life in pre-modern times, in the limited ways it is still available today. Visitors can travel to traditional villages in rural Turkey or India or China, sometimes even live with a family and immerse themselves in the pace and rhythms of times long past. One of the more enthusiastic tourism outfits I came across promises a greeting by villagers performing "traditional song and dance passed down from generation to generation," accompanied by "hypnotic beating of the tam tams." Visitors are assured that native people are "proud to share their heritage with you." In fact, we are told, "it is their simplistic lifestyle and inherent happiness that makes this tour so rewarding."[1]

This makes sense in a world that is by its very nature hypothetical, where anything we believe to be true — that Pluto is a planet or that a tomato is a vegetable — might be disproved at any moment. Social conventions once held sacred seem to have little traction. Men may hold doors for women, and churchgoers might dress up in their Sunday best each week, but fewer and fewer people will mind if they don't. If anything is set in stone these days, it is the quest for freedom from the smothering weight of arbitrary obligation, whether to the old country or to a particular brand of toothpaste. Every rugged individual worth his or her salt, from the lonesome cowboy to the Disney heroine, wants only escape from tradition, an open-ended freedom to become "myself," in whatever shape or form that may take.

Adding religion to the mix only complicates things further. Many of us automatically bristle at any "because I said so," especially when the bossy, nagging presence is God. Religious tradition brings to mind patriarchy and the suppression of women, racist beliefs and practices, and a blindly literal reading of the Bible. Most Americans, as survey after survey has demonstrated, prefer a god who is upbeat and helpful, knowing enough not to criticize someone who is trying very hard. Far more people, from across the religious spectrum, say they have experienced God's love than that they've worried about God's judgment. America's "comforting, avuncular God" is always reasonable, never too demanding.[2]

In reality, however, the central issue for most of us is not *whether* we have an obligation to anything larger than ourselves, but what form that obligation will take. We can say that we want

---

1. www.paradisetourssanto.com, accessed 11 August 2012.

2. Robert Putnam and David Campbell, *American Grace: How Religion Divides and Unites Us* (New York: Simon and Schuster, 2010), pp. 470-71.

to be free of arbitrary rules and regulations, but somewhere inside we know that will never happen. Twenty-first-century people accept far more restrictions in the course of our daily lives than our ancestors could have ever imagined. We follow the bidding of train schedules and clocks and stop signs as a matter of course, and are willing to wait in line for hours at an amusement park for ten minutes of mechanically orchestrated thrill.

Most people know at some level that the old ways are important, and they may even yearn for a way of life before the onset of plastic toys, television jingles, and junk food. The old ways seem to promise something more authentic and substantial than the endless vista of strip malls and fast-food restaurants we have created. But tradition is a complicated yearning. As much as it promises belonging and stability, it can also be deeply irritating, especially when it begins to impinge on individual freedom. It comes with a cost.

In this chapter we will explore this tension between belonging and independence, and the way it has complicated our relationship with the past. It is almost a commonplace that many Americans, and American churches, take their history and heritage far too lightly. We can point to any number of reasons why this is so, all rooted in rules of the modern world. But there is a twist: American religion itself is a major source of the problem. The way that Protestants in particular have learned to "do church" in this country has militated against a strong and nurturing connection to the past. It has kept us from participating in a great conversation that has been going on among Christians for more than two thousand years.

Historylessness

American culture is built on the principle of letting go and moving on. This is the personal story of millions of immigrants who still come here in search of something new and better, and the dream of every poor young mailroom worker hoping to die a millionaire. It is also the way we have learned to understand our own lives, as an open-ended journey of growth and progress toward better things. The idea of moving forward and throwing off unwanted "baggage" would have puzzled most people in the history of the world, but it is taken for granted on television talk shows and self-help books. Healthy people get over past wrongs so they can triumph over the adversities of life. Living in the past, we are reminded again and again, is a road to nowhere.

From its inception, the United States was a place for people who looked forward rather than back. The experiment in democracy was an astonishing move, all but unknown in the western world since the time of ancient Greece. The nation's founding represented nothing less than a *novus ordo seculorum*, a new order where history itself would start over. In reality the American Constitution drew on centuries of English civil law and the American people remained heavily indebted to their European cultural and intellectual heritage. But Americans took enormous pride in their freedom from the ossified ways of "old Europe," and declared independence in every possible way, from the organization of government to the subtleties of everyday speech. This is the reason why Noah Webster first published his famous dictionary. Americans might be still speaking English, the language of their oppressors, but they didn't have to do it in the same way. Webster's dictionary provided a simpler, homier American form of the mother tongue; extra vowels and consonants were fine for lazy aristocrats but a waste of time for the industrious self-made men of the new republic.

Our founding generations had little use for their own past. By the early nineteenth century, much of their history was literally gone; even famous places like Constitution Hall in Philadelphia, George Washington's estate in Mount Vernon, and Jefferson's Monticello were either remodeled beyond recognition or left to ruin. Paper records meant even less. On one notorious occasion in 1862 a casual bystander saved a major trove of important state papers from destruction when he happened to notice George Washington's signature on one of them. The documents had been stuffed into old tobacco barrels during the War of 1812, right before the British marched into Washington and burned down the White House. Fifty years later they were just piles of old papers sitting in the way of plans for renovation, and narrowly escaped a watery grave in the Potomac.[3]

Nowhere was the prospect of freedom from the past embraced more enthusiastically than in American churches. Just like democracy, American religious freedom was a "lively experiment," a complete break with everything that had come before. As far back as anyone could remember, religion had been the business of powerful people, led by popes and bishops and controlled by kings and queens and emperors. Ordinary people did not decide whether they would be Catholics or Lutherans or Calvinists; they went to churches with the official stamp of approval. Even the North American colonies for many years followed many of these same practices, with Congregationalism the established religion of New England and Anglicanism the only approved faith for Virginia. The separation of church and state in the United States Constitution was a startling departure from all these deeply-rooted practices. In theory at least, for the first time in history church membership was fully voluntary.

3. Michael Kammen, *Mystic Chords of Memory: The Transformation of Tradition in American Culture* (New York: Knopf, 1993), pp. 52-56.

More than that, American churches were also free from the limitations of time and tradition. Some fifty years ago historian Sidney Mead coined the term "historylessness" to describe this free-floating relationship with the past. In the emerging world of American religious diversity, with each church claiming to be the most faithful to God's plan, the brass ring of authenticity was a direct link to the first-century Christian church. Nothing that had happened over the course of nearly two millennia could ever improve on the original order set up by the first apostles. If anything, things had gone downhill since the rise of Roman Catholicism, which to most Protestants seemed a long and deliberate turn from the New Testament faith. The story of the early church in the book of Acts was the blueprint for the true church: the best faith was an original one, unsullied by two thousand years of history.[4] The actual nitty-gritty of the past, including all the people and events inhabiting the last two thousand years, was something to be leaped across, transcended rather than embraced.

This set of assumptions about the past still shapes the way Americans believe and behave today. In practical terms the power of the first-century model meant that religious institutions would be tolerated but not necessarily embraced; we prefer to keep our theological differences as hazy as possible. Denominational labels were especially problematic. In fact, some of the most ardent Protestants refused to take any name at all: one group of radicals simply called themselves "Christians," setting up unending layers of confusion for later generations of library catalogers and census-takers. Abner Jones, one of the leaders of the movement in New England, had become a Baptist during a revival meeting, but then, as he later reminisced, he decided to "believe and practice just what

---

4. Sidney Mead, *The Lively Experiment* (New York: Harper and Row, 1963), p. 111.

I found required in the bible and no more." "When I had searched the New Testament through, to my great astonishment," he said, "I could not find the denomination of baptist mentioned in the whole of it": neither Christ nor the apostles ever used the term, only referring to each other as fellow Christians. "After this examination I denied the name of baptist," he said, "and so I have continued to do until this day."[5]

Abner Jones's attitude still lives. It is one of the reasons for the popularity of nondenominational megachurches and parachurch ministries among American evangelicals, and for the increasingly low levels of denominational awareness among Protestants in general. The most successful new churches recognize that the average religious searcher is not pining to become a United Presbyterian or a Cooperative Baptist, but wants to find an open and welcoming community of faith. Abner Jones also lives on in the shrinking bureaucracies of mainline Protestant churches. For the past several decades social scientists have been predicting the end of denominations as we know them, arguing that they have become simply too big and expensive to maintain, especially as Americans gradually forget the reasons why they arose in the first place. No matter how the future turns out, however, the problem itself is hardly new. If anything, firm denominational loyalty is the more unusual mode for American Protestants – the fiery fundamentalist schismatic fighting over tiny points of doctrine has never been an ideal, much less popular, figure.

Historylessness has also helped Americans learn to tolerate religious differences. The bloody religious wars over baptism or the celebration of the Eucharist that had long marred European history mattered less and less on this side of the Atlantic, espe-

5. *Memoir of Elder Abner Jones, By His Son A. D. Jones* (Boston: William Crosby and Co., 1842), p. 28.

cially as people learned to make do under difficult circumstances. In eighteenth-century Pennsylvania, for example, German immigrants of all kinds, including Calvinist (Reformed) and Lutheran church members, settled in neighboring communities. In the centuries following the Protestant Reformation they had often ended up on extreme opposite sides; yet once in the New World the longing for a minister — any minister — trumped years of ancestral bloodshed. Henry Melchior Muhlenberg was a Lutheran pastor and evangelist who traveled many miles on horseback, preaching to any German church communities who would invite him in. On one occasion, as he later recorded in his journal, he addressed a large crowd made up of people from both sides of the old divide. "Several guileless Reformed people were sure that I was not a Lutheran preacher," Muhlenberg later wrote in his journal, "because I had not reviled and run down other denominations, but simply preached the order of salvation." The tolerant and non-sectarian approach apparently made quite an impression: one of his listeners walked all the way home "absorbed in sweet thoughts" before it occurred to him that he had left his horse standing by the church.[6]

As the nation's borders and its population expanded, the religious groups with the least historical baggage tended to be the most successful. The Methodist and Baptist evangelists who made first contact with isolated frontier settlements in the early 1800s had little in the way of accumulated wealth or ancestral ties to slow them down. Methodists in fact came with an extremely short history, as a group formed in the mid-1700s by the English followers of John Wesley. They did not even reach American shores until just after the Revolution. Baptists had been around longer, but mostly

6. *The Journals of Henry Melchior Muhlenberg in Three Volumes,* trans. Theodore G. Tappert and John W. Doberstein, vol. 1 (Philadelphia: Evangelical Lutheran Ministerium and the Muhlenberg Press, 1942), p. 299.

as a small and persecuted minority hovering around the fringes of Puritan New England. But age and wealth were not necessarily an advantage. As church-planting statistics show, older groups, including the Congregationalists in New England and Episcopalians in the Upper South, had trouble keeping up with the pace of church expansion. Encumbered with old buildings and deep community ties, as well as hundreds of years of history on American soil, they moved far more slowly, if at all.

The twentieth century, with its genocides and concentration camps, was a series of object lessons in religious and social tolerance, one that many American churches took very seriously. On the positive side were many years of successful cooperation between Protestants in evangelism and service for immigrants and the poor. Missionary work in particular broke down many old barriers of suspicion and conflict and built a spirit of ecumenical cooperation. In the wake of the Holocaust, the anti-Semitism long taken for granted by Christians could no longer be tolerated; even old enmities between Protestants and Catholics began to diminish. In fact, during the great humanitarian emergency of the Depression years and the horrors of World War II, many of those old differences seemed almost petty; putting them aside and working together seemed the only ethical thing to do. Narrow-minded fundamentalists might fight for their version of the "old-time religion," but the great needs of a world facing war and economic catastrophe required people of faith to forget the past and unite together in a common cause. Historical and theological niceties were for the small-minded, the bitter sectarian groups with a permanent grudge against sinners.

Today the pattern persists. The United States is one of the most religious nations in the world, with soaring levels of belief in God and in the power of prayer, but it is also one of the most tolerant — an achievement only possible because of the way we believe. A recent survey by sociologists Robert Putnam and David Campbell found that only thirteen percent of American adults think they have the corner on religious truth. These "true believers" are a small and atypical minority, even within the conservative evangelical churches where one would expect to find them. People like this, the stereotypical secularist nightmare, are vastly outnumbered by the eighty percent of American adults who agree that there are "basic truths in many religions."[7] Those figures are not likely to change, even in the post-9/11 world. If anything, the lesson of that day was the danger of religious intolerance gone unchecked.

All in all, the acceptance of other people's beliefs is a remarkable achievement, what researchers Putnam and Campbell call the amazing "American grace." But it has also imposed a cost. For many people, history is an obstacle in the way of tolerance; in order to work properly, our system requires short memory spans. History brings up old and unnecessary conflicts, the reasoning goes, and tiny irrelevant quarrels that once rekindled could prove impossible to control. This assumption was at the bottom of many denominational mergers in the twentieth century. My own denomination, the United Church of Christ, was formed in 1957 when four different bodies came together in what was hoped would be a model for the Christian church in the future. The leaders of this union recognized very clearly that "faith" was going to have to "[take] precedence over history." The great need of the world, as one of them declared, "challenges the denominations of our day to justify the perpetuation of their cherished traditions – however hallowed they may have become." Genuine Christian freedom meant breaking free of the "fetters of history," he insisted, hoping that the "overtones of faith" would drown out

---

7. Putnam and Campbell, *American Grace*, pp. 541-47.

"the lingering undertones" of the past.[8] I write this not to single out any group — "historylessness" knows no denominational boundaries — but as an example of the false choice American Protestants seem to have accepted. Today we believe that one can be religiously tolerant *or* loyal to a particular denomination or set of theological beliefs, dangerously sectarian *or* gracefully unaware of the past.

This choice is not only unnecessary, but an unaffordable luxury. If anything, our cultural orientation toward the future is growing stronger and accelerating quickly; historical traditions are on the defensive as never before. All kinds of statistics and studies have shown that the 1960s were a time of "great disruption" in social attitudes and moral values. Social scientists and historians are still debating about the cause — the Cold War, hippies and drugs, the feminist movement, Richard Nixon, or the rise of television — but no one can deny that the 1960s brought deep and lasting social changes.

Those "earthquake years" also upended American churches and synagogues. First of all, the baby boomers, those born in the 1950s and early 1960s, stopped going to church in astonishing numbers — according to one set of polls, from over half in 1957 to just over a quarter in 1971. Though many of them inched back into church once they married and became parents, many others did not. Since the 1960s the numbers of Americans without any religious attachment, what sociologists call the "nones," have mushroomed. From just 5 percent of the World War II generation, the proportion of "nones" has grown to 25 percent of the generation coming of age in the 1990s and early 2000s.[9] This group is not necessarily atheist or even agnostic. They are simply uninterested in

8. Carl E. Schneider, "The Crisis of Faith and History," *United Church Herald*, 9 June 1960, pp. 18-19.

9. Putnam and Campbell, *American Grace*, pp. 97-98.

religion – and their children will likely carry on and intensify that pattern as they grow up and become parents themselves.[10]

What will happen to the chain of religious memory? Even the simple practical issues involved in keeping track of the past are becoming more complicated and crucial. When a local church closes or merges with another, unless someone makes a commitment to sort through years of old paper, decades and sometimes centuries of history can be lost. Among mainline churches, denominational bureaucracies and the libraries of theological seminaries have usually taken the main responsibility for preserving old records and artifacts. But when a stressed institutional budget demands sharp cuts, the archive staff and the historical society do not easily take precedence over immediate social needs. The parachurch organizations and independent megachurches that now dominate the religious landscape are not likely to develop strong institutional memories either. Especially in these days of constantly expanding – and instantly deletable – electronic communication, any kind of consistent record-keeping is an enormous challenge.

These problems won't be solved by infusions of money or better policies, by more hard work or louder shouting; what's needed is a mature and thoughtful understanding of the past itself. We have seen how the modern world has eroded connections to our ancestors, placing us at the far end of history with few good reasons for reaching back. This does not mean that change is impossible and history is a doomed project. It simply means that we should refuse old and unexamined assumptions about the irrelevance of the past, and think seriously about the ways it applies to the present and the future. We can begin by turning to the question posed at the beginning of this chapter: what is the purpose of the past and its traditions for people and communities of faith?

10. Putnam and Campbell, *American Grace*, pp. 121f.

A Usable Past

Confusion about the meaning and purpose of tradition is everywhere. It transcends theological differences between religious liberals and conservatives and crosses every denominational boundary. Rootless religion is as much at home in the seamlessly inoffensive worship of a mainline church as it is in a slick and shiny suburban megachurch. In each case the past has no weight, especially when it might conflict with the demands of the future. Within this vacuum, any convictions can assume enormous power. Some of the most traditional people I have ever met were members of extremely liberal denominations, weathering inclusive language without a wince but prepared to fight to the death over the picture on the front cover of the bulletin.

To some people the past is a blueprint: the beliefs and practices of the founders are mandatory guidelines. Just as a plan for a house will never end up producing a supermarket, so the reasoning goes, a group of orthodox Calvinists will never produce New Age flower children. If the Founding Fathers were evangelical Christians who prayed at the Constitutional Convention, then we should be too. If the founders of a religious tradition did not use musical instruments in the worship service, then we should not either. Anything else is a fundamental betrayal of the founding vision.

Traditionalism — for this is really what we are looking at here — does not really connect people with history, despite its claims. The past is not a still photograph but a movie, and it is very difficult to mark one cel of film as the most important. In other words, more times than not the founders of a tradition are hard to identify. Certainly they did not wake up one morning and decide to start something utterly brand new — most often they thought they were insiders making a few adjustments to fix some important problems. Martin Luther never called himself a Lutheran, Menno

Simons a Mennonite, or John Calvin a Calvinist. Over time, as
the surrounding culture changes, the teachings of the founders
change too. In fact they can become so obscured by the arguments
and misunderstandings of later generations that they are all but
impossible to recover. Which of us can say what defines a "true"
Mennonite or Roman Catholic or Pentecostal? Over the past several centuries all of these have meant many different things to different people.

But treating tradition as if it were completely arbitrary is not
the solution. For some people the present is just one of a million
possible trajectories from the past, and the future just as unknow-
able. It is as if all of the work of the past, all of the convictions and
desires of thousands of people, has no real traction.

The simpler and more human view, the one that resonates the
most with the biblical and Christian tradition, is that the present
unfolds organically from the past, like an oak tree grows from an
acorn. Even though they are not identical — an oak tree is not a giant acorn — there is a genuine and necessary connection between
the two. How to understand that organic connection is the burden
of the rest of this chapter.

Both traditionalism and anti-traditionalism put history to use
for present-day agendas, whether preventing change or pushing it
in a certain direction. This is not to say that history can't be useful — there is no doubt that knowledge of the past illuminates the
world today in all kinds of important ways — but it does not *stop*
there. History is not optional, something that we can decide to use
or not use; it can be a matter of literal life and death.

Examples are distressingly easy to come by. I think immediately of the treatment of Indian tribes in the late-nineteenth century, as they were pushed from their own lands onto government-
sponsored reservations. During a time of rising violence on the
western frontier, as droves of pioneers and gold-seekers spread

across the mountains and plains, sequestering Native Americans from settlers seemed like a good idea. Not only would this policy lower the possibility of war, but also allow the government to "pacify" Native Americans by requiring them to speak in English, take up farming, and cut their hair. Instead of following the old ways, under the Dawes Act of 1862 the tribes were to adopt Christianity and send their children to boarding schools, where they would learn to "adapt" to modern civilization. Though intentions behind this idea were a complicated mix of cultural insensitivity, greed, and sincere compassion, the result was a long, slow disaster, the effects of which we still see today. Those old ways were the glue that held families and tribes together and gave individuals meaning and purpose; they were the central logic behind an entire way of life. Instead of opening the door to civilization, the destruction of the old led to widespread anomie, alcoholism, and despair.

Something similar happened to the slaves brought to North American shores from Africa. The brutality of the Middle Passage across the Atlantic Ocean and forced separation from family and tribe were damaging enough, but in the long run the loss of African cultures proved the hardest to overcome. One of the great questions about slavery in North America is the almost complete absence of older religious beliefs and customs. Slaves in the Caribbean and South America somehow managed to create blends of African and western traditions in religions like voudun and Santeria. But not in North America. Here historians have looked long and hard for evidence of African "survivals," and found plenty — but the fact that they had to search for them testifies to one of the central tragedies of American slavery, and one of the reasons for its long and painful legacy. People without an anchor in their traditions of the past have far fewer protections from the present.

It is easy to sentimentalize the "plight" of Native Americans and slaves, and of all tribal people who find themselves in the path of progress – but that misses the real point of their stories. Though these travesties of justice should make the rest of us grieved and angry, that does not mean we have the luxury of pity. These are also stories about us, as people of faith living the modern western world.

All of us have lost something important, a meaningful continuity with the past. Although we have no real language for mourning this loss, we are also becoming unglued from religious traditions which at one time provided connection with something larger and more important than ourselves. At best we complain and worry about "secularization" and the way its unseen forces have destroyed all that is good and holy. Other times we blame church leaders and Christian educators for not standing up more emphatically for their core beliefs, for quietly giving in instead of resisting at every turn. But neither alternative really points the way toward a solution. What we need is to recognize the ways that religious faith has been narrowed and changed as the western world has modernized, and to see this loss for what it is. Rather than yearn for a religious golden age or impose tradition as a way of shoring up the sagging walls of our religious institutions, we can begin a new round of conversation about the past, present, and future of faith in a clear-headed, thoughtful, and creative way.

The Great Conversation

At its heart, a religious tradition is a long conversation. It is not a set of beliefs or practices set in stone for all eternity, nor does it exist just to give our religious institutions a reason for continuing on. Nor are traditions a set of funds in a bank account ready to be pulled out every twenty-five years or so for an anniversary celebration. They have been created by people for other people.

More than that, they are conversations about *something*. The Christian tradition itself is a long conversation about the declaration that "Jesus is Lord." We might also say, just for the sake of argument, that the Mennonite tradition is one about the witness of the godly community; for Methodists it might be the issue of holiness, and for Baptists the implications of conversion and immersion. Calvinists wonder about the sovereignty of God and what this means in belief and practice. Some religious groups organize their questions into confessions and creeds, statements of faith drawn from the Bible. Major Protestant denominations – Lutherans, Presbyterians, Dutch and German Reformed Churches, and Scots Covenanters – turned to the Augsburg Confession, the Westminster Standards, or the Heidelberg Catechism as a way of helping ordinary people understand the essential message of the Bible. That does not mean that these statements are infallible, but they are not simply antiques for display either. They are meant to spur serious conversation.

At a dinner party or a classroom or a church meeting, a lively conversation is diverse and dynamic. New people can enter in with different perspectives and different levels of understanding of what has been going on. They might stay for a while, or drop out. At times certain voices will be dominant, shouting down other points of view – but they may well end up replaced by others. From time to time the conversation shifts in mood: it can be spirited or contentious, playful or serious. It could even be slow and dull. And it might also generate side-discussions, some lively and flourishing and others slowly dwindling into silence. But here is the crucial point: a conversation is not a verbal free-for-all, where anyone can come in and shift the subject to something completely different. The talk always circles and weaves around a central topic.

This is how traditions stay relevant and compelling. We will never understand our faith by "progressively sloughing off more and more of tradition," historian Jaroslav Pelikan writes, "as though insight would be purest and deepest when it has finally freed itself of the dead past." A truly creative conversation builds on what has been said before, exploring nuances and suggesting different interpretations – but never assuming that the people who began it have nothing more to say and can be safely ignored. The living do not own the conversation any more than those past or those yet to come. In fact, "[b]y including the dead in the circle of discourse," says Pelikan, "we enrich the quality of the conversation."[11]

Here our metaphor can get tricky. Exactly which dead people are we talking about? We are rightly suspicious of anyone who is one hundred percent sure what the conversation should involve and who should be allowed to participate. For many thousands of years, the Christian churches excluded women almost entirely. Some argued that, as the descendants of Eve, women were the willing victims of deception, while others excluded women because they were deemed too delicate and emotional to think straight. No matter what the argument, the point was the same: the Christian tradition was a conversation among men, and preferably white men with lots of education. When women began to enter in (very recently and in some cases still not yet), things got uncomfortable and confusing – people were speaking different dialects and shouting at each other as if that would make their meaning clearer. To some it looked like the orderly talk had broken out into anarchy. But to many more people the conversation suddenly became more interesting. Unexamined ideas went on trial, and though they were sometimes sentenced to exile or imprisonment, in other cases they emerged tested, affirmed, and vindicated.

11. Jaroslav Pelikan *The Vindication of Tradition* (New Haven: Yale University Press, 1984), p. 81.

Growing Up Traditional

I sometimes tell people that I know the answer to every third question in the Heidelberg Catechism. I should explain: In the Dutch Calvinist tradition I grew up in, this statement of faith was the central talking point in every religious gathering. I remember hearing many sermons on the questions and answers of the catechism; I listened to my parents and their friends discuss them; and when I reached fifth grade, I had to begin memorizing them. This was not something I welcomed. Our elderly pastor would come to my school on Monday afternoons and conduct a class for the children of church members; I would listen anxiously for the sound of his dentures whistling, a signal that he would be wrapping up soon. Each week we were to memorize three sets of questions and answers, and his pedagogy consisted of going around the room in order, up one row of desks and down the next, and having each student recite one of the three. My strategy was to sit far enough back in the classroom so that I would be able to calculate which answer I would have to know, and also have enough time to cram it into my short-term memory. The plan was risky and it often failed me. Invariably someone ahead of me would stumble and the order of the questions would change instantly, as would my game plan.

I can't say that this was an ideal religious upbringing, but many years later I realize its particular gift. Over time I received a clear set of ideas about the Christian faith, a kind of mental structure of belief. Some of the ideas were troubling and some interesting, and some incomprehensible — but they were ideas to argue with. By the time I finished high school I had the makings of a lifelong spiritual project.

I was reminded of my catechism days when I was asked to review a book about women in conservative religious communities. These were members of very conservative Jewish and Roman

Catholic communities who not only stayed within those synagogues and churches but sent their daughters to religious schools
there. All of these mothers were highly educated women in professional careers who clearly wanted their daughters to be strong
and self-sufficient. But they also believed that this required taking religion seriously, and this meant making it uncomfortable.
Simply imposing a set of beliefs would never do, for the mothers
or for the daughters, nor would leaving it all up to fate. These
"appropriately subversive" mothers, as the author of the study
called them, relied on their religious communities to set the rules
– regulations about clothing, going to movies, and the like – and
then took the role as the mediating voice of reason. The mothers
were realistic: they knew that their daughters would rebel some
day, but they wanted them to do it wisely and well. As one Jewish mother explained, she wanted her daughter to make a true
choice, not just run away from religion. "If you don't know anything about anything," she said, "then you don't have anything to
choose from." And so while these mothers and daughters would
have some epic conflicts, the arguments were at least always interesting. They were *about something.*[12]

Our religious traditions are more than blueprints or points
on an infinite trajectory. The choice is not to load our ancestors
down with honors or run away from them as fast as we can – our
countercultural faith requires us to take the past seriously and to
receive its people warmly and wisely. It requires us to be generous,
and in a fundamental way truly inclusive.

British author G. K. Chesterton describes tradition as "the democracy of the dead." The living – a "small and arrogant oligarchy
. . . who merely happen to be walking about" – cannot abuse their

12. Tova Hartman Halbertal, *Appropriately Subversive: Modern Mothers in Traditional Religions* (Cambridge: Harvard University Press, 2003), p. 125.

power by disenfranchising "the most obscure of all classes, our ancestors." We should invite the dead to our councils and "vote by tombstones." After all, says Chesterton, true democrats "object to men being disqualified by the accident of birth; tradition objects to their being disqualified by the accident of death."[13]

13. G. K. Chesterton, *Orthodoxy* (New York: Dodd, Mead and Company, [1908], 1959), p. 48.

CHAPTER FIVE

The Communion of Saints

On my way to work, I walk past a large graveyard. This is not as grim as it might sound, though I am sure some of my Calvinist ancestors would appreciate my daily reminder of mortality. This particular cemetery is surrounded by miles of old stone walls, about chest high and intricately draped with grapevines and ivy. On the other side of the wall, underneath tall shady trees, hundreds of people lie buried beneath a hodgepodge of weather-beaten monuments. The gently rolling landscape of this cemetery looks for all the world like an upscale city park, which of course it was built to resemble.

Sometimes when I'm walking home in the dark, I edge toward the other side of the street; I'm not superstitious, but sometimes their looming presence can be too much for my imagination. In the early morning, however, the cemetery is genuinely peaceful, empty except for an occasional jogger or a few people walking pets, slipping furtively past the signs that say "no dogs allowed."

From time to time I wonder about the people buried there, and how their lives ended. I can picture a family in Victorian dress laying to rest a tiny infant or parents saying final farewells to a son killed in battle. I can guess that some of the grave markers were erected for abusive fathers or neglectful mothers, some for people who were deeply mourned and others for those barely missed.

There's great mystery in that cemetery, even deeper than the painful or tragic events that populated it. Inside its stone walls are the citizens of my town: they built the stores and mapped out the roads, put up electric lights, founded the hospital, and organized the public library. A few probably lived in my house at one time. They have made my life possible in more ways than I can count, yet we are entire strangers.

After a crowded subway ride into Boston and another short walk up Beacon Hill, I arrive at my desk and look out over yet another graveyard. The Congregational Library backs up onto Boston's Granary Burial Ground, the final resting place of many famous people — Paul Revere, Samuel Adams, the victims of the Boston Massacre, and rumor has it even Mother Goose. From early March through the end of October it is a busy, sometimes even noisy, place. Knots of exhausted tourists and gaggles of hyperactive middle schoolers cruise the aisles behind tour guides in colonial dress, whose high-decibel spiel I have long since memorized.

Everyone stops at the graves below my window. My closest neighbor is Paul Revere, one of my childhood idols (and by some cruel irony my day is regularly punctuated with warnings that "the British are coming!"). Few visitors look further, at the ragged, crowded rows of more ordinary folk, many of them entire families laid to rest side by side. In fact, despite the high-profile celebrities in the Granary Burial Ground, the vast majority of the people buried there exist to us as only a few words on a gravestone, now all but erased by wind and weather. Determined researchers can uncover broad details of their lives through baptismal registers and town records — but no one will ever know the inner stories of their lives, why they chose their marriage partners, what they talked about at night after a long day of work, their talents and skills, quirks and habits.

I do not take these silent neighbors for granted either. Sometimes, when all of the library staff have gone home, the lights are off, and I'm working alone at my desk, I think about them, I have to admit. I force myself not to turn too quickly, and if I'm walking in the stacks, I try to avoid idle glances down empty hallways. It would make perfect sense for a stray Congregational ghost to indulge a little nostalgia with a visit to our library.

But most of the time, my feeling is more sadness than fear. It is hard to think about people who have lived full and eventful lives, only to end up as a faded name on a monument; it is even harder to realize that this will eventually happen to me and to all the people I love. My library shelves are full of forgotten books written by unknown people. It is an amazing fact, one that I sometimes contemplate with awe, that all of these books are connections with people now on the other side of mystery, surviving only as a name on a tattered binding. That's one reason why I sometimes pause and say their names out loud, just to give the universe a chance to hear an old and beloved combination of words one more time.

This chapter is about the Christian doctrine of the communion of saints. We affirm in some fashion the presence of those saints every time we recite the Apostles' Creed – in fact, right after we declare our belief in two doctrines we think about a great deal, "the resurrection of the body" and "the life everlasting." But most of us don't dwell on this one overmuch. Maybe we're not entirely sure what it means. Maybe we don't realize that we're talking about a relationship with the dead.

Inevitably, in a book about the past, death is going to come up. Granted this may be a fairly morbid topic for some, but bear with me. The assumption that the dead have nothing to do with the living – and that the living need not worry about the dead – is another reason why there is so little historical traction in our world today. The way we remember those who have lived before says volumes about the way we view the past and its meaning for the present.

Saints Alive

Some historians say that modern individualism got its start when the dead were banished from the world of the living. And if we were going to pinpoint an exact moment when this occurred, we could not do any better than Martin Luther's protest against the Roman Catholic doctrine of purgatory. Most people are familiar with the story: in 1517 Luther, an Augustinian monk, took on the notorious Johan Tetzel, a Dominican preacher who was selling indulgences in Wittenberg. These were certificates which would reduce the time of suffering for those who had died with unconfessed sins, and allow them to make quicker progress from purgatory into heaven. The English translation of Tetzel's tagline (which one historian has called "the most infamous jingle in all of Western history") is also familiar: "When the coin into the coffer rings, the soul from Purgatory springs."[1]

The Protestant Reformation was an event of enormous sweep and power. It shook European society inside and out, from its political alliances to its philosophical underpinnings, reorienting belief and practice in ways that still rumble across the Christian world. Tetzel was selling indulgences to raise money for a new basilica in St. Peter's Cathedral in Rome, problem enough for Luther and the people of Wittenberg. But indulgences also symbolized everything that Luther felt was wrong with medieval theology, suggesting that salvation was possible by following the rules of the church rather than by faith in God.

One of the biggest challenges is one we often overlook, however. Luther's protest, which soon spread across northern Europe, was against the entire Roman Catholic system of masses and pen-

1. Carlos Eire, *A Very Brief History of Eternity* (Princeton: Princeton and Oxford University Presses, 2010), p. 106.

ances and last rites. And in that sense, the Reformation would sever a connection that ran deep in the history of Western European Christianity, the obligations of the living to the dead.

From its earliest days, Christianity was known for the strength of this invisible tie. The religion of the Mediterranean world was "upper worldly," as historian Peter Brown describes it. The realm of the divine sat "above the moon," in "the untarnished stability of the stars," and beneath it the earth like "so many dregs at the bottom of a clear glass." Death was the soul's final release from this darkness and decay into the realm of airy perfection. The Christian doctrine of the resurrection ran emphatically counter to this idea: Christ came back to life both body and soul, and instead of returning to the void, he returned to encourage and instruct his friends and disciples.

Yet in an odd and somewhat paradoxical way, the tomb became an important symbol for Christians, "not in order to sacralize the burial ground," says writer Robert Pogue Harrison, "but to recall its ultimate vanity." The real message was the angels' announcement on Easter morning, "he is not here."[2] The early Christians took to gathering in cemeteries, touching and sometimes even embracing bodily remains of holy people — relics, they called them — as pagans recoiled in horror. Not only did those Christians claim to be drinking the blood and eating the flesh of Christ; according to eyewitnesses, they "collected the bones and skulls of criminals who had been put to death for numerous crimes." To the Romans' disgust, Christian worshippers "made them out to be gods" and martyrs, "and thought that they became better by defiling themselves at their graves."[3]

---

2. Peter Brown, *The Cult of the Saints: Its Rise and Function in Western Christianity* (Chicago: University of Chicago Press, 1982), p. 2; Robert Pogue Harrison, *The Dominion of the Dead* (Chicago: University of Chicago Press, 2003), p. 110.

3. Quoted in Brown, *The Cult of the Saints*, pp. 1-2.

The connection strengthened further within the structure of medieval Catholicism. From its archaeological remains, we can see that the Roman Catholic Church rested quite literally on the dead. Cathedrals grew up around the shrines of saints, and relics were built right into their walls. Over time, the dead were an integral part of European community life — and in fact an entire economic system. Historians have calculated that masses for the dead, indulgences, relics, and pilgrimages accounted for a huge part of church fundraising. In 1529 an English Protestant complained to King Henry VIII that belief in purgatory had placed more than a third of his realm under the control of the clergy. The English cardinal William Allen agreed that the doctrine of purgatory had "founded all Bishoprics, built all Churches, raised all Oratories, instituted all Colleges, endowed all Schools, maintained all hospitals, set forward all works of charity and religion, of whatever sort soever they be."[4]

The Protestant Reformation did away with all of this: not just popes and indulgences but funeral masses and relics and prayers to saints. "The expression 'dead and gone' acquired a new meaning among all Protestants," says historian Carlos Eire, "for once dead, one was literally whisked to either heaven or hell, to realms totally beyond the reach of living humans." The Reformers themselves practiced what they preached. Before he died, John Calvin instructed that his body be buried in an unmarked grave outside the walls of Geneva. His friend Theodore Beza recounted how the crowds began to gather as news of Calvin's death began to spread, hoping for a glimpse of the holy man's body. "Many strangers had also come earlier from far away to see him . . . dead as he was, and applied to do so." But to prevent such "calumnies" Calvin was carried to the cemetery "without any pomp or show whatever," and

4. Eire, *A Very Brief History of Eternity*, p. 125.

there "he lies now, awaiting the resurrection he taught us about and so constantly hoped for."[5]

The separation was physical too. In European Catholic churches, the dead were buried in the "churchyard," a kind of sacred space around the building; those of higher status were even buried in the walls of the sanctuary itself. After the Reformation Protestant cemeteries became known simply as burying grounds, places with far more practical than religious significance.

The New England Puritans were especially emphatic about discouraging excessive mourning and ornate funerals. Ministers refused to preside at those ceremonies, except perhaps to read a Bible passage or two when the family was together. The dead were to be "decently attended from the house to the place appointed for publique Buriall," as one Puritan writer explained, "and there immediately interred, without any Ceremony." Fancy funerals were more than just a silly waste – they were "in no way beneficiall to the dead," and "have proved many wayes hurtfull to the living."[6]

I see the results of this conviction every time I walk from my office to the subway. The Granary Burial Ground beneath my window includes many people who were long-ago members of the Old South Church, established in 1669. But, as a good tour guide will tell you, the Granary is not part of the church's property, nor was it reserved for Old South members only. It is a "burial ground," blocks away from where the original church was built. People who want to visit an actual churchyard can go down a block to the King's Chapel, built for the Puritan-hating royal governor. There

5. Eire, *A Very Brief History of Eternity*, p. 123; Beza quoted in Bernard Cottret, *Calvin: A Biography*, translated by M. Wallace McDonald (Grand Rapids: Eerdmans, 2000), p. 262.

6. *A directory for the public worship of God*, quoted in David E. Stannard, *The Puritan Way of Death: A Study in Religion, Culture, and Social Change* (New York: Oxford University Press, 1977), p. 101.

they will find all kinds of important folks within the building's shadow — though, again as any good tour guide will also tell you, a good many of them were members of Boston's First Church, gathered in 1630 and located another several blocks away, carefully distant from its dead.

Over the years churches and cemeteries drifted further apart. By the early nineteenth century critics were complaining that town burial grounds were a disgrace: bodies were being left in unmarked graves and rarely tended. Cemeteries were becoming overgrown and unkempt, downright depressing. During this romantic age, when nature seemed a friend and the human soul full of good, social reformers campaigned for new ways to remember the dead. The park-like space I walk by on my way to work was in fact their ideal. Almost every city seems to have at least one or two of these, meant for contemplative strolling under shady trees and by picturesque ponds. Usually there is a small chapel somewhere on the property, a place for holding a small nondenominational ceremony. But the overall effect of the cemetery is quietly nonsectarian. The goal of these beautiful places was to help people come to terms with the finality of death in a gentle and comforting natural setting.

More and more, ceremonies around death took place in homes instead of churches. The people buried in the cemeteries that frame my daily routine would probably have died in their own beds and then been washed, dressed, and "laid out" in the family parlor as relatives and friends gathered for the funeral. Death itself would have been part of a familiar pattern, certainly no less painful than it is today, but far less secretive and private. More well-to-do families would call in a photographer to take formal pictures of a dead child, as she or he was laid out in a coffin in white burial dress. In fact, during this time mourning rituals grew more and more elaborate, to the point where we would call them unhealthy.

Not only did Victorians build those beautiful cemeteries, they remembered the dead with mourning rings and lockets, sometimes incorporating strands of the deceased's hair into the design.

Protestant churches seemed to have less and less to offer during times of bereavement. For many people of the nineteenth century, who had gone through the Civil War and its enormous human toll, the answer was spiritualism, a complicated mix of faith and fraud, promising direct contact with friends and relatives in the Great Beyond. Although today séances and mediums and rappings in the dark are considered a fringe interest – not something you would witness in the ordinary American living room – they were enormously popular a century and a half ago. Scratch the surface of nineteenth-century Victorian culture, and very soon you'll come across a floating table or mysterious automatic writing forming on a page. It's not hard to imagine that these signs of the supernatural provided comfort to grieving widows and orphaned children – a kind of direct comfort that Protestant churches were usually reluctant to provide. In a broad sense, since the Reformation, Protestantism was a faith for the living, not the dead.

It is during our time that the dead have begun to disappear in earnest. Lengthening life spans, the increasing availability of hospital care, and a burgeoning funeral home industry have brought dramatic changes to the relationship between the quick and the dead. Most of us will witness few actual deaths in our lifetimes, and we certainly won't have the experience of washing and laying out the body of a loved one. This is now the job of licensed professionals. The "intimacy that had connected the physical remains with a community of family and friends," one historian writes, "was being supplanted by a gaping social divide." In keeping with this trend, cremation became increasingly common in the late twentieth century. All but unknown in American culture to this point – and as late as 1963 associated with only four percent of deaths – cremation was the chosen option in one quarter of American funerals in 1999.[7]

Interpreting this trend requires some care. The turn toward cremation instead of burial does not mean that people stopped caring about loved ones, or that they wanted to dispose of them with a minimum of trouble. The practice has a long and honorable history. In ancient Israel, Greece, and Rome, and in Buddhism, cremation was a way of demonstrating respect for the dead, of releasing the imprisoned spirit from the burden of physical flesh. In American culture, however, as historian Stephen Prothero writes, the switch toward cremation signaled something much more significant than personal attitudes toward dead people. Twentieth-century American death rituals were changing to follow the direction of the culture itself. They were learning ways to deal flexibly with both the physical remains of death and with memories of loss.[8]

Defending the Defenseless

In 1939, a week before the invasion of Poland, Adolf Hitler gave his military staff a history lesson. "It was knowingly and lightheartedly that Genghis Khan sent thousands of women and children to their deaths," he said. But what were the consequences? History does not see him as the mass murderer he was. He is remembered only in terms of what he accomplished, as "the founder of a state."

The same was true in the last World War, said Hitler. A million

7. Gary Laderman, *Rest in Peace: A Cultural History of Death and the Funeral Home in Twentieth-Century America* (New York: Oxford University Press, 2003), p. 1; Stephen Prothero, *Purified by Fire: A History of Cremation in America* (Berkeley: University of California Press, 2001).

8. Prothero, *Purified by Fire*, p. 5.

Armenians died in a systematic campaign of ethnic annihilation led by the Turkish state, an event later named as the first genocide in human history. They were killed by firing squad, bayoneted, bludgeoned, and starved, men and women and children alike. But the terror was mostly invisible to the outside world. Despite fervent protests from eyewitnesses, most of them missionaries and diplomats stationed in Turkey, American and European leaders all raised good common-sense reasons for keeping their distance. The old Ottoman Empire was an ally of Germany in the war, a creaking powder keg of a country – not one that the rest of Europe wanted to rile if they could help it. For its part, the United States turned its back on the Armenians because it was trying to avoid getting involved in a European quagmire. And so the government-sponsored genocide continued on, eventually becoming lost in the horrific death toll of the Great War itself.

"Who today still speaks of the massacre of the Armenians?" Hitler demanded of his officers. Taking a lesson from the past, he assured them that the siege of Poland would bring no long-term consequences. In fact, in 1942, at the height of World War II, Hitler restored the ashes of Mehmed Talaat, a Turkish interior minister killed by an Armenian assassin, to their native soil. The two men shared a common bond as leaders of bloody campaigns of ethnic cleansing, but they also knew a shameful truth about human character: the world's unwillingness to remember the first genocide would always enable the next.[9]

Memory requires a community. Elie Wiesel is an eloquent voice on the moral imperative of "never forgetting" the horror of the Holocaust, and the systematic, cynical, calculated way so many people were killed. In refusing to forget, we share in their

9. Samantha Power, *"A Problem from Hell": America and the Age of Genocide* (New York: HarperCollins, 2002), pp. 1-23.

suffering and form a "shield" for the voiceless and the weak. Remembering, as a large and determined effort, is the only salvation, says Wiesel, from future atrocities. And it takes on meaning when we are able to stand up and remind each other that we are not immune: *we* are the kind of people who do these terrible things.

The dead occupy an ambiguous role in our society today – they are here and yet they are not here – and as a result we are not always sure of our commitment to them. Certainly they outnumber us. In 2002 demographer Carl Haub estimated the total number of people who have ever lived on earth at 100 billion – which means that we, the 6 billion alive today, make up a tiny sliver (6 percent, in fact) of the human race. If life on earth were a democracy, we would be outvoted every time.[10] Of course the dead are not people in the way we ordinarily use the term, as individuals with consciousness and the ability to act. But they once were. The fact that they are now "less than human beings" but "more than objects" means that we cannot just shunt them aside.[11]

Respect for the dead is a rule in every human culture – one reason we feel instinctive horror over discoveries of mass graves or desecrations of cemeteries. Even in our future-oriented world we do our best to document the exact time a person dies and to record their name and dates of birth and death on tombstones. No one looks forward to being left in an anonymous grave or a "potters' field." Our laws protect their wishes in perpetuity, as these were recorded in wills and bequests. Even where there is no legal issue,

10. Carl Haub, "How Many People Have Ever Lived on Earth?" *Population Today* 30:8 (November/December 2002): 3-4.

11. Antoon de Baets, "A Declaration of the Responsibilities of Present Generations Toward Past Generations," *History and Theory* 43 (December 2004): 130-64. De Baets argues for an international agreement that would parallel the human rights laid out in the Geneva Convention.

you or I would find it enormously difficult to sell Aunt Susan's beloved china collection or give away her cats to a shelter. In some
way we feel that the dead still deserve our protection. We keep
their secrets and protect their privacy long after they are gone. And
if they are victims of violence or genocide, we know there is an
obligation to right those wrongs.

The ambiguities of death have become even more profound in
our digital age. The dead speak to us in saved voicemails and video
clips; we can send them emails and post messages on Facebook
pages. Computer-generated avatars in games like World of War-
craft or Second Life still keep their hoards of virtual weapons and
money. Our blog posts, musical creations, tweets, pictures, and
status updates will live on in cyberspace long after we have ceased
to care about them. Not surprisingly, forward-looking entrepre-
neurs are beginning to offer advice for "digital after-life manage-
ment" and dealing with the "digital litter" left behind on blogs and
websites. In the future, you or I may want to name a digital execu-
tor, to keep embarrassing emails or Tumblr sites from destroying
our posthumous reputation, and to preserve the thoughts, images,
and ideas that we would want for our long-term legacy.[12]

In a way, though, the ambiguities are not as great as we think
they are. The dead seem more than able to fend for themselves. To
those who stop to look, the invisible ties which bind one generation to the next pop up everywhere. In fact, in my various travels to
local churches I have seen, over and over again, exactly how powerful those silent ancestors can be. Take for example my encounter
with a mid-sized church in a seafaring town, celebrating its three-
hundredth anniversary. The pastor there had written a lengthy
history of the church, a detailed account but so colorful that I read

12. Rob Walker, "Cyberspace When You're Dead," http://www.nytimes.com
/2011/01/09/magazine/09Immortality-t.html, accessed 5/16/2012.

it in one sitting. By the time I was finished, however, I began to worry for his safety. The pastors of that church had drowned with depressing regularity — and not just in the ocean, as one might expect, but in lakes and rivers and streams. Sometimes they fell off boats and sometimes they just disappeared in the midst of a swim. It seemed to me that the church should be issuing life preservers to new pastors at each installation service.

And then there were other stories. I visited one 350-year-old church that, I happened to know, had recently dealt with sexual scandal involving the pastor. I also knew that it had been organized in the early 1600s under somewhat dicey circumstances, with a pastor exiled from Boston under the shadow of heresy. As the years passed, the church seemed to skirt the edges of propriety with surprising regularity — and I don't mean just theologically. This was one local church history I wanted to put back onto the shelf in a plain brown paper wrapper.

I do not mean to suggest some kind of weird determinism behind the complex dynamics of those congregations' histories. But I do believe that the past plays an important, often unarticulated role in creating present-day realities. This is why we spend hours with therapists and counselors, hoping to distill some useful truth from an inventory of our life experiences. But the invisible power of the past is also true in human groups, and especially so in communities of faith. Year after year, as new members join a church and children come of age in the Sunday school, they accept a certain understanding of "who we are" and "why we are together." So much of this has to do with the circumstances of a church's origins, often long buried but still real. It makes a difference if a congregation was born out of angry controversy and schism, or as the result of a miraculous outpouring of the Holy Spirit. Sometimes in the founding of a church the overriding current of emotion is pride, and in others it can be frustration or even despair. Knowing at least something about those original circumstances is important, whether they go back fifty years or three hundred. The ancestors live on in different ways, sometimes as a deep undercurrent of sadness or disappointment, sometimes as a tendency toward suspicion of outsiders or resentment of authority. They can work in positive ways too, inuring a centuries-old congregation against instant panic or despair. All of this suggests the importance of getting to know the "communion of saints" who created and shaped the spiritual values, strongly held beliefs, and even personality quirks we think are ours alone.

Writer Miroslav Volf explains this more poetically. We experience time, he says, the way we hear a beautiful note from a cello. It may sound like a single pitch, but in reality it is a complex tone, including other voices from the string's half-length, fourth-length, eighth-length, and so on. "It is similar with the music of our lives," says Volf. "At any given time we do not hear only the simple, solitary tone of the present; rather, in that present resonate many sounds of past actualities and future possibilities. This is how our present acquires depth."[13] In other words, our present-day lives are constantly echoing those of others.

The Communion of Saints

What are we to make of that phrase in the Apostles' Creed, "the communion of saints"? It is not something that comes up all that much in the normal process of "doing church." Perhaps it seems a bit superstitious to imagine ghostly figures flying around the sanctuary on Sunday morning, whispering hymns and prayers along-

---

13. Miroslav Volf, *The End of Memory: Remembering Rightly in a Violent World* (Grand Rapids: Eerdmans, 2006), p. 73.

side us as we sit in our pews. Or maybe it conjures up unpleasant possibilities of angry ancestors shaking their fingers at us modern-day sinners, sighing heavily when we launch into upbeat praise songs and muttering with disgust when we use inclusive language. But in fact the communion of saints is an idea that grows more compelling as we begin to unpack its history.

Scholars tell us that this phrase was a relatively late addition to the creed. It floated around in some different versions until the early fifth century, and became a permanent part of the creed when it took its present form in the early 700s. (In spite of the title, the creed was not written by the apostles themselves.) They point out that there is no mention of the communion of saints in older and more widely used statements of faith, including the Roman and Nicene Creeds.

Perhaps because the phrase was not nailed down as early as some others in the Apostles' Creed, it took on different meanings. The grammar of the Latin phrase suggested to some that it referred directly to the sacraments: the *communio sanctorum* was the church's "participation in sacred things," the waters of baptism and the bread and wine of the Eucharist. The other understanding was a little less scholarly and much broader in scope: the communion of saints included the entire "invisible church," the believers on earth as well as the angels, saints, and martyrs in heaven. These ideas did not really contradict each other – it was possible to recite the creed with either or both meanings – and so the ambiguity remained until the time of the Protestant Reformation. By then it was ripe for reinterpretation.[14]

As we have seen, the Reformers had little use for saints or for either of the traditional explanations of the phrase in the Apostles'

14. Arthur Cushman McGiffert, *The Apostles' Creed: Its Origin, Its Purpose, and Its Historical Interpretation* (New York: Charles Scribner's Sons, 1902), pp. 200-204.

Creed. They emphatically opposed the idea that the Church had control over "sacred things." The sacraments were God's free gift to the people of God, not privileges doled out by the clergy. The idea of a communion of saints also ran directly against the Reformers' emphasis on the living rather than the dead. The blessed dead "do not abandon their own repose so as to be drawn into earthly cares," Calvin argued; "and much less must we on this account be always calling upon them!" For Protestants, then, the communion of saints referred to the assembly of living believers. The phrase was not a stand-alone idea, suggesting something mysterious and metaphysical, but simply another way of saying the "holy catholic (universal) church." The word "communion" could be used interchangeably for "church" or "congregation."[15]

Recovering the original meaning of the phrase — as nineteenth-century historian of Christian creeds Philip Schaff argues, "the Fellowship of all true believers living and departed" — does not mean going back to the days of relics and indulgences.[16] Nor does it require us to figure out all of the imponderables that may come to mind: the exact location, itinerary, and appearance of those dead believers, or the particular theological qualifications for belonging to the communion of saints. I don't mean to make light of these: many gifted minds have spent lifetimes trying to sort out biblical passages dealing with the afterlife and the End Times, or the means of salvation. Those are important questions, but they take us outside the simple idea we are working toward: that all of God's people — past, present, and future — form a single, interdependent whole. Together all the

15. John Calvin, *Institutes of the Christian Religion*, ed. John T. McNeill (Philadelphia: Westminster Press, 1977), pp. 882-83. Wolfhart Pannenberg, *The Apostles' Creed In the Light of Today's Questions* (Philadelphia: Westminster Press, 1972), p. 149.

16. Philip Schaff, *The Creeds of Christendom, With a History and Critical Notes*, vol. 1 (New York: Harper and Brothers, 1877), p. 22.

"families in heaven and on earth," as Paul describes them (Ephesians 3:15), make up the body of Christ, the invisible church across the ages.

The author of Hebrews gives us an even more startling metaphor: a "cloud of witnesses," standing around us and cheering us on as we "run the race set before us." This famous passage also defines faith as "the assurance of things hoped for, the conviction of things not seen." I imagine that at least some of those "things not seen" are the biblical people named in the rest of the passage: from Abel and Enoch to Abraham and Moses. All of them — the heroes of Jewish history, the women who received their dead by resurrection, and martyrs who endured torture and imprisonment — are near and available to us, not just as role models, but as companions and guides.

This makes sense in several ways. Most of us are tempted to skip over the long genealogies in the Gospels or the endless lists of tribes and sub-tribes in the historical books of the Hebrew Scriptures. They are certainly not devotional reading, at least in the obvious sense. But those passages, and this long list in Hebrews 11 and 12, are built on the conviction that individual lives are important. It is pretty remarkable that thousands of years later we know the names of some fairly obscure people, people who were not "historically important" in the way this is usually understood. Not everyone in the list of saints is all that saintly either. The list includes Rahab the prostitute, Samson the man conquered by his lust for Delilah, and Jephthah, the judge who sacrificed his own daughter to make good on a promise. The communion of saints is not a cloud of perfection or an undifferentiated mass of the living and the dead, but something far more incomprehensible: the infinite array of personal experiences and convictions, talents and achievements, sins and failures that make up the human race across time and space.

Chapter eleven concludes with the somewhat odd statement that these people of faith "did not receive what was promised." God had provided something better, "so that they would not, apart from us, be made perfect." For a long time commentators assumed that this phrase was referring to the people of Israel, suggesting that at the end of all things they would finally be saved through the blood of Christ. This "triumphal" interpretation of the passage suggests that only the Christian faith is a truly perfect one, through which the heroes of Israel would be in a sense retroactively converted from Judaism.

But this is not the only possible interpretation. The passage may also be read "humbly," as one commentator suggests, recognizing that the people of Israel "lived the earlier chapters of one continuous story" that we are still finishing.[17] We do not redeem Abraham and Moses, and we cannot make them perfect. Instead, through the "high-priestly ministry of Jesus Christ" we are all part of "a great unbroken record of faith stretching from the beginning of human history all the way into the heavenly sanctuary of the city of God, where the cord has been securely fastened and anchored by Jesus."[18] This is a phrase that underlines not just our interdependence with other Christians but our spiritual solidarity with all the people of God, past as well as present and future.

In one sense we are all unique, absolutely one-of-a-kind individual creations; but in a much more profound way, each of us has come about as the result of a "long choosing." This is a phrase from writer Wendell Berry, whose book *Remembering* describes Andy Catlett's struggle with a sudden bout of amnesia. To those familiar with Berry's stories about Port William, Andy is a familiar figure,

17. *Hebrews: The New Interpreter's Bible*, vol. 12 (Nashville: Abingdon Press, 1998), p. 147.

18. Thomas Long, *Hebrews: Interpretation, A Bible Commentary for Teaching and Preaching* (Louisville: John Knox Press, 1997), pp. 126-29.

having grown up in the town's rich web of family and neighbor-hood relationships. His disorientation begins during a confusing and painful trip to a scientific conference, where he is caught up in the security lines and body searches now a familiar part of the post-9/11 world. In this world, every stranger in an airport terminal is a potential enemy, someone to be kept at a safe distance. When Andy makes it back to his home in rural West Virginia, he is in rough shape. His memory and his sense of self return only when in a confused dream state he reconnects to his ancestors. To Andy they are a "long dance of men and women behind, most of whom he never knew, some he knew, two he yet knew, who, choosing one another, chose him." Andy Catlett is not a self-made man liv-ing in an isolated blip of a town, but he and his home are the sum of hundreds of courtships and conceptions, choices and chances, errors and hopes.[19]

We like to imagine that we are unique, absolutely unprec-edented. But here is the truth: not just the tilt of our noses or the color of our bodies, but far more intimate characteristics – the shape of our feet or an inner tendency towards joy or sadness – have belonged to other people before we came along to inherit them. We came about because they decided to marry one person and not the other, to have six children instead of three, to move to a city instead of staying on the farm. It is remarkable to think of someone walking down the streets of sixteenth-century Amster-dam with my fingers and kneecaps, my tendency toward melan-choly and my aptitude for music.

We live within a web of holy obligation. We are connected to people of the world today, and to those who created the world with their own labor. We are also connected to other invisible people:

19. Wendell Berry, *Remembering: A Novel* (Berkeley: Counterpoint, 2008), p. 50.

the unknown number of generations yet to be born. One of the most important things we can do, in the way we care for the earth and in the way we care for our local church life, is to recognize their potential presence. And in the next and final chapter, we will take up the last big question: how can remembering become part of our daily practice? What does Christian remembering look like?

CHAPTER SIX

The Spiritual Practice of Remembering

All this time, that old and battered tricorne hat has been sitting quietly in its Plexiglas case, still posing its question: why? If we temporarily bracket out sentimental reasons and ask the question in pragmatic terms, the alternatives are pretty stark. On the one hand, the thought of tossing a centuries-old hat in the garbage – or even the more humane alternative of donating it to the church rummage sale – is offensive, if not downright appalling. Somehow the hat deserves to spend its retirement years in a more dignified way. But on the other hand, the reasons for preserving it are not all that clear. Does posterity need an eighteenth-century hat? It has no practical value and probably wouldn't even bring all that much in an antiques auction. So why is it – and really all the flotsam and jetsam of the past – still here?

By now we understand why this is such a challenging question. As people of our time and place we carry a load of assumptions about the past, all of them telling us that things "before" have nothing to do with the present or the future. We believe that time moves in a straight line, always inching forward. Once the past is over, for us it is gone forever. We also believe that the people before us are behind us, and have little to offer our twenty-first-century troubles. In fact, we are almost tempted to treat them as figments of the imagination. Perhaps our view of the past is so contaminated with our biases and misperceptions that it is impossible to know events and people as they "really were." At the bottom of the deep well of time, all we can see are our own faces reflecting back.

In plain, practical terms, then, it doesn't matter what we do with the stuff of the past. Its owners are long gone and any meaning it once held has long since drained away. It is nice to keep around as a curiosity, but utterly irrelevant to life in the present.

But we don't have to think this way. It is also true that the Christian faith offers points of connection with the past, different ways of staying in vital conversation with our ancestors. In fact, our religious traditions come with an endless array of talking partners, people from the past who might challenge or delight us, frustrate or anger us — but are still speaking the same language of faith. None of us in this old, old conversation have more or better truth than the other; we are not higher on the chronological ladder of enlightenment than our ancestors. We are simply part of the same communion of saints, God's people spread across time and space, who need each other to "perfect" our faith. We are not isolated from the past or forever stranded in the present — we are surrounded by a cloud of witnesses.

In this sense, the act of remembering is rich with possibilities. In this chapter we will explore some of these, and imagine what Christian remembering might look like in practice, how it might shape us into mature and thoughtful people of God.

Re-membering

We know a great deal today about how the mind stores memories. What was once imagined as a store of file cabinets is actually a series of intricate chemical and psychological mechanisms, all operating at lightning speed. In fact, the more complexities scientists discover, the more awe-inspiring it all seems. When we search for a memory, the entire brain goes to work; new and sophisticated imaging equipment shows different and highly specialized parts of the brain communicating with each other, working together to retrieve an image of an event or person. Scientists have also linked certain kinds of memory with different parts of the brain; remembering answers on a test is a vastly different chemical process than something more automatic, like riding a bicycle or breathing. Recapturing a memory, in other words, is a shared task requiring highly sophisticated biological coordination. This means that there is no one place in the brain responsible for storing memories; even on the level of biochemistry the act of remembering is a cooperative effort.[1]

What better metaphor for our spiritual practice? Christian remembering begins with the assumption that all of us — past, present, and future — are joined together in a web of obligation. No one has a corner on the truth: we do not reach back for a single authoritative view of "what happened" or "what God was doing" at a particular time. We are after a much more textured version of the past, one much stronger than any individual memory can provide. In a profound sense, memory is a process of "re-collecting" and "re-membering" scattered people.

At the center is a remembering God. We often think of God as outside of human time, existing somewhere in an endless realm of eternity. But in fact, in Judaism and Christianity both, God shares our bonds of memory. How else to explain all the reminders to God not to forget? "Remember your covenant with us," the prophet Jeremiah pleads, "and do not break it" (Jeremiah 14:21). "Remember the people you purchased of old," the psalmist urges (Psalm 74:2). On one level

1. For a more detailed description, see Daniel Schacter, *Searching for Memory: The Brain, the Mind, and the Past* (New York: Basic Books, 1996).

it seems surprising, if not a bit presumptuous, to prod God's memory this way. Doesn't the Holy One know how to keep promises? But the idea of God remembering — of going back over time to the events of the past — does not mean God might forget us. It means that remembering marks us as people of God. It means that God is part of the long choosing, the same long story that defines our lives.

This is why memory kept the people of Israel together through times of doubt and discouragement. The Hebrew Scriptures are honeycombed with God's commands to "remember the days of old, consider the years of ages past" (Deuteronomy 32:7). Over and over psalmists reminded the people of Israel to keep in mind "the wonders [God] has done," from the miracles of manna and water running out of a rock in the desert to the certain judgments awaiting sinners (Psalm 105:5). God also asked the Israelites to remember difficult times — "that you were a slave in Egypt" (Deuteronomy 5:15; 15:15; 16:12; 24:18) — and that their deliverance had required painful sacrifice from others. "Remembering Zion" during times of exile brought tears of misery, as the people of Judah hung up the harps and wept by the waters of Babylon (Psalm 137). The purpose was not to wallow in regret or what-might-have-beens. The past was important because remembering brought hope and confidence; God was there in the past as God would be in the future. "My soul is cast down within me," the psalmist declares, "therefore I will remember thee" (Psalm 42:6).

Memory unites Christians as well. Christ's great command to his disciples at that famous Last Supper, which Christians all over the world repeat every time they celebrate the Eucharist, is to "*remember* and believe." Since those early days, there has been more disagreement and conflict over the meaning of the Lord's Supper than unity around it — some Christians see it as a reenactment of Christ's death, and others believe it is mostly symbolic. But the central point is still the sacrificial love of Jesus Christ. When we "remember and believe," as one commentator puts it, we are "pleading guilty" to the brokenness of our world, and joining to be agents of God's forgiveness and restoration — taking our place as members of the human race and as children of God.[2]

Biblical remembering not only creates a bond between people; it also integrates body, mind, and soul. Remembering is more than a mental activity — it requires action. Israel is to "remember the Sabbath day and keep it holy," and keep the laws of God always in mind. Christians are called to "help the weak, remembering the words of the Lord Jesus" (Acts 20:35). This memory centers the whole person, body and spirit alike, in commitments to do the right thing. When we "remember the poor," this means not letting individual concerns blot out other people. When we remember Jesus, we are no longer isolated individuals but part of a dynamic community of memory. Another way of saying this is that we are recognizing that we part of the communion of saints, a gathering of Christians that reaches back to those first years in Jerusalem and forward to the burgeoning new churches in places like Seoul, Lagos, and Buenos Aires.

This is not necessarily fun or easy work. Meeting God in the past may well shake some things we always thought were true. One congregation I know of had a painful encounter with this truth and the memories of a long-ago quarrel that led to a rancorous split. Everybody thought they knew the story: the members who left were malcontents, unwilling to cooperate or compromise. Their departure was their own choice and their absence a blessing to the rest. This meant that those who stayed on — including their descendents in the present-day congregation — were the righteous remnant, embattled but pure.

2. Allen Verhey, "Remember," in *The Anchor Bible Dictionary*, Vol. 5, ed. David Noel Freedman (New York: Doubleday, 1992), p. 669.

Unfortunately, the legend did not hold up to the facts. All of the tidy assumptions came to an abrupt halt when someone in the congregation began to study the past in earnest, including the story of that long-ago split. Instead of an angry walk-out by thickheaded ideologues, the church controversy was actually about a group in power banishing those who disagreed with them. Instead of a righteous remnant, the present-day congregation was the descendant of a self-righteous oligarchy. They were the kind of people who had once let the church split rather than allow dissenting views.

And so this congregation has its own special ritual of remembrance. When a meeting threatens to become too hot and people start talking over each other, someone walks over to the door and gives it a good loud slam. The gesture is a warning, a reminder that in the past anger had forced some members out of the fellowship – and that it could happen again. Instead of breaking apart over difficult memories, this congregation uses them to come together.

Traveling Light

Among the wide offerings of reality television, the most disturbing programs have to be those about hoarders. These are people, usually living alone, who are unable to part with anything, from junk mail to cats to rotting food in the refrigerator. Over time their houses become completely overrun by stuff, making it impossible to sleep in any of the beds, eat from the kitchen table, or even reach the back door. Sooner or later family, friends, and even local police and fire department have to intervene: the house is not only a hideous place for a person to live, but a fire and health hazard for the entire neighborhood.

Obviously this kind of behavior points to a serious psychological problem. People whose houses are overrun with cats are not

just animal lovers with a special passion; they are emotionally unable to part with even one scrawny kitten. When the Animal Control people come to call and find cats pouring from the closets and
covering the kitchen floor, the poor soul in the middle of the mess
is bereft and confused, openly frantic over the impending loss.

I suspect these shows are popular because in some mysterious
way they are about us. We are as confused as any hoarder about
what is important to keep and what is not. "Big box" stores and
supermarkets are filled with things we don't need but can't resist
taking home – and more than often end up piling up in basements
and closets, filling up landfills and garbage dumps. Never before,
as historian David Lowenthal points out, have museums and ar-
chives been so filled with "stuff" on display. The possibility now of
digitizing vast amounts of paper and reducing it to a single electronic file means that old limitations of space are gone. We now
have digital collections of important historical records for scholars to read from anywhere in the world – but also millions of old
postcards and photographs of no particular interest to anyone. Our
fear of forgetting is the engine behind most new personal technology: complicated devices that take care of relatively simple things
like doctors' appointments, birthdays and anniversaries, and the
way from here to there.

Of course there are plenty of good reasons to keep old things.
An old photograph or faded sweater helps us feel connected to
someone who has died, or it keeps alive the memory of an important day. We display odd objects in museums and libraries because
they are interesting and often fun to look at. We preserve the furniture of famous people because in some way this honors the people who once owned them.

But let's be clear about our motives. It's not just forgetting the
past we worry about – sometimes, I think, we are afraid of the
ancestors themselves. In that case old hats and postcards and but-

tons serve as talismans to ward off angry ghosts, invisible figures threatening to wreak vengeance if we do not take proper care of their stuff. At bottom this kind of keeping without remembering is a form of superstition, trying to protect ourselves from evil by keeping all those objects in their proper place. It has nothing to do with Christian faith.

In the Christian tradition, the essence of remembering is traveling light, making wise choices about what is important and what is less so. In both the Roman and medieval worlds the basic meaning of piety *(pietas)* was indebtedness, as in a careful respect for the legacies of the past. A true Christian reverenced the ancestors and their great acts of faith and, even more than that, was committed to keeping those memories alive. Conversely, forgetting was associated with "laziness, softness, and laxity." People who made no conscious effort to know and honor their ancestors were by definition pursuing a "low or merely pleasure-seeking mode of life."[3] But remembering was never an end in itself, a pious form of ancestor-worship. A sanctified memory allowed Christians to choose the good over the bad, the ways of God over the ways of the world. To the great teacher Aquinas, the discipline of prudence *(prudentia)* was impossible without a "well-furnished memory." The larger the memory stockpile, the more likely a wise and godly path; a paltry store of knowledge and experience would only lead to trouble. This is perhaps why many of the great saints of the faith were noted for miraculous feats of memory: St. Francis, it was said, could recall every event in his life since childhood, and St. Anthony could recite the entire Bible after simply hearing it read aloud. This was not the kind of remembering associated with parlor games or memory

3. David Gross, *Lost Time: On Remembering and Forgetting in Late Modern Culture* (Amherst: University of Massachusetts Press, 2000), pp. 28, 29, 30.

THE SPIRITUAL PRACTICE OF REMEMBERING

contests; saints had great powers of recollection because they were close to God.

In Christian tradition, remembering and forgetting were decisions with moral consequences. This is certainly true when it comes to the grace of forgiveness, of being willing to treat the other as if the wrong had not happened. It includes a positive commitment to restoring broken relationships and making things right. But in an even more specific way, Christians have seen forgetting as a way of deepening a primary allegiance to God, a way of clearing the ground for spiritual growth. In the monastic tradition, for example, novices were required to forget everything about their previous lives, not just the fading trivia of their daily to-and-fro, but even the details of their personal biographies. The purpose of this disciplined forgetting was to make room for what was most essential, the love and magnificence of God. According to the Rule of Benedict, "there must be both *oblivio* and *semper memoir*, that is, one must forget the ephemeral" in order to travel light, "to achieve a more intense and all-consuming remembrance of the eternal."[4]

None of this happens automatically. At the most basic level, we meet our spiritual debt to the past by paying attention – like that famously frightened little boy in the movie "The Sixth Sense," we must start "seeing dead people." This does not mean stopping the car every time a historical marker hoves into view, nor are we talking about clanking chains and floating bed sheets. What we are after requires far more imagination than that. Like all spiritual practices, Christian remembering is not a set of duties or list of skills to master – it is an intention, one that begins with the simple grace of noticing.

Once you begin to look, the past is everywhere: the roads that our ancestors built and the trees they planted, their songs and

4. Gross, *Lost Time*, p. 52.

books and pictures and monuments. Whether you live in an old New England town or a shiny new suburb, on top of a centuries-old Spanish settlement or in a constantly changing urban landscape, they are still present. Their inventions make us more comfortable on a hot day and happier when the weather gets cold. Their tastes and style, their sense of order and place, define our surroundings. Whether we realize it or not, we are living in a world they built and are bound to their decisions – as our children and their children's children will be to ours.

Noticing is unhurried and careful work. In fact, it is all but impossible while speeding around in a car or flipping pages across the Internet. I came to understand this in a new way when I pedaled my bicycle on a route I had taken many times by car. Roads I once assumed were perfectly flat suddenly became long uphill slogs; that particular stretch where I had always pushed my toe a little harder on the accelerator became an exercise in grit and perseverance. But when I reached the top I knew that road with an intimacy I hadn't before – and in a more truthful way. I would no longer take my accelerator for granted.

This kind of unhurried awareness makes it possible to feel a connection, perhaps even a sense of gratitude, to those who imagined, laid out, and paid for the buildings and houses and streets of my town – even the ones going uphill. Those other people made sure that there would be open space and trees, churches and hospitals, mail delivery and electricity. Some might find it a little odd to say a general thank-you as you are walking by something wonderful, but it would not be out of order to do so.

Of course, gratitude will not be our only emotion: many of the leavings from past generations will rightly make us frustrated and impatient, perhaps even angry. Our ancestors have left behind long legacies of racial hatred, foolish wars, and wholesale destruction of the natural world. They winked at injustices that in our day have exploded into bloody revolutions. As much as we might enjoy their accomplishments, we are also trapped in the messes they knowingly or unknowingly created. Because of them the people of God are called to remember terrible things – wars and holocausts and crusades all done in the name of religion.

In fact, the commitment to notice the past in our surroundings takes some nerve and determination – it is profoundly countercultural. The anonymity of suburban housing tracts and urban high-rises, superhighways and airports, may keep us safe and sane at times, but it also imposes a spiritual cost. These places have no history, which makes it difficult for the people in them to remember theirs.

But there are ways to fight back. In a city neighborhood I had lived in for many years, people began to tack homemade historical plaques on buildings and street signs, snippets of information about those places and why they were important. Once I stopped and read a few, I discovered that some were "historical" in the strict sense, about famous people or events associated with a particular spot, and others were personal. Some identified a house as a former dry goods store or soap-maker's cottage. Others described a tumble off a bike that happened in front of that house, a breakup with a boyfriend at that playground, or even a mugging that took place at that street corner.

What an interesting experiment. I lived in that neighborhood for years without knowing I was a few blocks away from the former home of the Boston Strangler. Now, through the experiences of others, I began to really know it. The thin layer of my life in one house on a particular street began to take on depth and dimension. If anonymous, faceless cityscapes are "the way modernity forgets," then telling the human stories behind them is a way we might begin to remember.

Something even more complicated happens when communities of faith begin to build a repertoire of memory. I can imagine, for example, a church building covered with do-it-yourself historical markers. Some of these might identify old family friends or relatives as donors of stained glass windows or parlor rooms, or explain why that depressing portrait is still hanging in the Sunday school hall. Notes on the pulpit or the baptismal font could offer memories of a life-changing sermon or family ritual; notes on pews could provide reminders of other church members who had claimed that particular piece of sacred real estate in the past. I can imagine memory notes in every part of the church, from the kitchen to the communion table, turning empty modern walls and furniture into sacred space.

Some of those notes will be hard to read. I cannot imagine a church building that does not resonate with unhappy and painful memories. The toxic past has great potential for collateral damage and, at the very least, it leaves a sticky mess for others to clean up. Certainly some of those memories reflect a lifetime of self-pity and narcissism, of people too small to let go and forgive. But with others anger might well be justified, defying any attempt to let bygones be bygones. All of this underlines the necessity of approaching the past with caution and respect. It is not just a fading figment of the imagination; it demands all the honesty and spiritual creativity we can muster.

Keeping

For all our worries about divine providence and God's will, the really hard part about history is accepting the humanness of the past and its people. Just as there are no one-dimensional heroes and villains in real life today, there were none 200 or 2,000 years ago either. All of us live somewhere between fear and hope, sharing the precariousness of life on planet earth. But we learn to understand our situation within different cultural ground rules and different physical limits.

Our ancestors are on the one hand terribly alien to us, yet we are also profoundly connected to them. They confront us with the full span of human diversity, in beautiful, frustrating, and challenging ways. We do not need to excuse them for their various sins and omissions, treating them as if they came from some wildly exotic civilization. We have the right – and the responsibility – to disagree and complain and rail against them within the framework of our common tradition, that extended argument constantly unfolding across both space and time. Even though they do not literally talk back, it is still possible to learn to hear their voices clearly.

Without our ancestors, we can't really know what it is to be human. Some linguists argue that the Latin word for human (*humanitas*) is related to the word for burying (*humando*). In other words, it's not a stretch to say that to be human is to bury our dead – and, even more important, to remember where they are. Archaeological evidence suggests that the earliest hearths and the earliest homes were built over those ancient graves.

Humanitas is also related to *humus:* in other words, being human means possessing a deep, rich soil, layers and layers of all that has gone on before we were born. This is the kind of soil that makes life out of dead things, that connects them in a cycle of fertility and growth. We are, after all, born of the dead, taking over their physical space, their languages, and their ideas – and we are the ones who will hand these over to our unborn. We the living are a ligament between the generations, the only connection between what was long ago and what is yet to come.[5]

5. Robert Pogue Harrison, *The Dominion of the Dead* (Chicago: University of Chicago Press, 2003), p. x.